The Image of Progress

ALABAMA PHOTOGRAPHS, 1872–1917

The Image

of Progress

ALABAMA PHOTOGRAPHS, 1872–1917

Melton A. McLaurin and Michael V. Thomason

THE UNIVERSITY OF ALABAMA PRESS · UNIVERSITY, ALABAMA

The Image of Progress
by Melton A. McLaurin and Michael V. Thomason
was typeset on a Mergenthaler 606
in Bookman 444 text and
ITC Bookman display
by Akra Data, Inc., Birmingham, Alabama.
Book design and page makeup by Anna F. Jacobs

Library of Congress Cataloging in Publication Data
McLaurin, Melton Alonza.
   The image of progress.
Bibliography: p.
Includes index.
1. Alabama—Social life and customs—Pictorial works.
2. Alabama—Economic conditions—Pictorial works.
3. Alabama—Description and travel—Views.
I. Thomason, Michael, joint author. II. Title.
F327.M32   976.1'061'0222   80-11441
ISBN 0-8173-0043-0

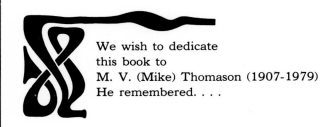

We wish to dedicate
this book to
M. V. (Mike) Thomason (1907-1979)
He remembered. . . .

Contents

Acknowledgments vi

Preface vi

Introduction 3

The Economic Setting 17

The Social Setting 123

Bibliographic Essay 215

Index of Photographic Collections 219

Acknowledgments

We wish to acknowledge the help of many people in preparing this manuscript. None is more deserving of credit than Mr. William Brantley, who found and copied prints in Bay Minette and Greenville and helped with much of the photographic research in Mobile as well. Throughout the state, archivists, librarians, and staff personnel made us welcome, opened their collections to us, and helped in many ways.

Special thanks are due to Mrs. Carter Smith, Historic Mobile Preservation Society; Mr. Curren Farmer, Pike County Museum Association; Mr. Bill Summers and Dr. Allen Jones, Auburn University Archives; Dr. Marvin Whiting, Birmingham Public Library; Mr. Daniel T. Williams, Tuskegee Institute; Ms. Elizabeth Wells, Samford University; Mr. William H. Leary, National Archives; Mr. Wayne Love, G. S. Houston Library; and Mr. Caldwell Delaney, Museum of the City of Mobile.

The manuscript was typed by Ms. Colette LaCaruba, Secretary, History Department, University of North Carolina at Wilmington, and by Ms. Margaret Robberson, Official Court Reporter, Mobile County Circuit Court. Professor Carole Fink, University of North Carolina at Wilmington, offered useful advice on the manuscript, as did several other historians in Alabama. The Reference Department staff of the University of South Alabama Library, especially Ms. Kathy Jones, also helped us in many ways.

This book would have been impossible were it not for the pictures made by the New South photographers themselves. Although we do not even know all their names, we acknowledge our debt to them and our gratitude for their work.

Finally, we thank our families for their support in this project and their tolerance of our obsession with it.

Preface

Photography has fixed an image of Alabama and the South in the mind of America. At times the camera has revealed the virtues of Alabama's people, among them the close family ties, a deep religious faith, and a strong sense of individualism. But from the days of the New Deal's Farm Security Administration photographs to the 1960s images of Robert Frank's *The Americans* or Bob Adelman's *Down Home*, a widely held, unflattering image of the state has emerged. The devastation of sharecropping, the pervasive racism of Southern life, the poverty of the region's people, and the exploitation of the Southern worker have all been recorded by some of America's best photographers. Walker Evans, Dorothea Lange, and other professional photographers revealed the grim truth about Alabama during the Depression. Countless photojournalists came to the state in the 1950s and 1960s to record the struggles of the civil rights era, and for over a decade their photographs were seen on the pages of the national press. Their work reinforced for the nation and the world an essentially bleak view of the state and region.

That image of Alabama was uncomfortably accurate so far as it went. Indeed, both photographers and historians have suggested that the South exhibits openly some of the darker sides of the American psyche, that it is less unique than honest. Southerners did not hide from the lenses of outside photographers either their Depression woes or their bitterness over the civil rights revolution. But the image the photographers created was incomplete. They had focused on the region's problems largely because in an era of the mass media its problems were newsworthy.

The impact of modern photography upon Americans' perceptions of Alabama raises questions about the role of the camera in recording the state's history. What do we learn from photographs taken before the Great Depression and the civil rights movement catapulted Alabama and the South into national prominence? In the era labeled the New South, from Reconstruction to World War I (1877–1917), many photographers worked in the state. Their surviving negatives are as revealing of that time as the photographs of Walker Evans or Bob Adelman are of a later period. Unlike the post–World War I photographs that shaped the nation's perception of Alabama, the work of New South photographers was not influenced by the needs of the press because photojournalism was then in its infancy. As a result, their work covers a broad range of subjects and presents a wide-ranging, complex, and generally sympathetic view of the state.

By the end of the nineteenth century many towns in Alabama had at least one professional photographer, and such cities as Mobile and Birmingham each had eight or ten studios. In every city, town, and village "part-time" professionals or amateurs practiced the art. Little of their work has survived, however, and for most of them we know no more than their names and business addresses. Sources of information are few; advertisements in local business directories, obituaries, and infrequent newspaper articles provide most of what is available. In Mobile the five most important photographers of the era—Albert Sandoz, William A. Reed, Charles H. Mader, William E. Wilson, and Erik Overbey—were all immigrants. Birmingham's J. F. Knox, on the other hand, hailed from Belt Buckle, Tennessee. Some of the negatives made by all these men, except Sandoz and Mader, survive.

Whether native-born or not, the photographers of the New South were essentially businessmen imbued with the attitudes and values of their era. Alabama was emerging from the old plantation South, and its photographers were eager to grow with it and to record that growth. Though some were more financially successful than others, most were practical men who appreciated the patronage of the rich and influential. Their work indicates that Alabama's photographers accepted their patrons' equation of growth with progress. After all, their pictures were made to sell, whether they were portrait or commercial work. Yet despite ideological and financial constraints, the early photographers produced a visual record of the life of almost every segment of Alabama society.

Of the pre–World War I negatives that survive, most are studio portraits and the work of professional photographers. Although some of Alabama's amateur photographers turned to film negatives after 1900, professional photographers generally used glass negatives until the eve of World War I. Most used 8- by 10-inch plates in ungainly tripod-mounted cameras. The apparatus was heavy and cumbersome and the glass negatives required long exposures by modern standards. Nevertheless, some photographers, like William E. Wilson of Mobile, often got out of the studio. Others, like Roland Harper, a geologist at The University of Alabama who worked with a homemade box camera, had no need for a studio at all. Most, like Reed and Knox, concentrated on a studio setting whether they were working with individuals, families, or fraternal groups. Taken indoors or out, the reality of the New South comes through in their photographs, as does the photographers' acceptance of the world as they found it. These photographs are as revealing of the values of Alabama's people, of their relationships to one another, and of their relationship to the physical landscape in which they lived and worked as are any taken since.

The majority of the photographs taken in Alabama during the New South era undoubtedly have been lost. Some were destroyed when photographers died or went out of business; others fell victim to fire, flood, or simple neglect. Still more deteriorated to the point of uselessness because of poor storage conditions or improper initial processing by the photographer. Less than a century later, few negative collections have survived in Alabama. Yet the collections that did survive are particularly important. They include a greater variety of images, and the negatives they contain are generally larger and thus include more detail than prints. Negatives also allow a higher quality reproduction with modern materials than do the surviving print files. Most negatives are 8- by 10-inch in size; some are 5- by 7-inch; very few are smaller. They require little if any enlargement to produce prints. By comparison a modern 35-mm negative is routinely enlarged eight to ten times. The results are acceptable but do not compare with the tonality and sharpness of a contact print of an old negative.

There are five large negative collections in the state. The collection in the Auburn University Archives has over 40,000 negatives, most of which portray Birmingham after the turn of the century. The collection includes J. F. Knox's work as a portrait photographer along with negatives and prints that chronicle Auburn University's growth. The University of Alabama houses a second body of negatives, all the work of Roland Harper. Although carefully catalogued, these glass negatives are primarily of geological or botanical subjects. Many are missing, notably those of cities, towns, and factories, thus making this large collection of comparatively little use to the historian. By contrast, the Tuskegee Institute's collection of negatives and prints is of great value, for they show us the work of that institution in a variety of areas. The photographs of A. P. Bedeau, Frances B. Johnston, and others also provide a view of the life of black Alabamians in rural areas surrounding Tuskegee, and for this reason alone they are extremely valuable because such material is difficult to obtain.

The other two substantial negative collections are in Mobile, the state's oldest city, and include images from the 1870s through the 1960s. The smaller of the two, the William E. Wilson Collection of the Historic Mobile Preservation Society, is perhaps the more interesting because of the variety of subjects it contains. Wilson, who documented most aspects of life in Mobile from 1895 to 1906, left beautiful glass plates that are now well organized. The Erik Overbey Collection, which contains roughly 90,000 negatives, is housed in the University of South Alabama Photographic Archives. It includes negatives by William A. Reed, who began work in the early 1870s. Shortly after his arrival from Norway in 1903, Overbey purchased some of the Reed negative files. Like the Auburn Collection, the Overbey negatives are primarily portraits but they also contain hundreds of street scenes, views of the port, and shots of numerous other subjects, including Mardi Gras celebrations. The University of South Alabama Photographic Archives also contains two smaller collections, the T. E. Armitstead Collection and the Barnett Collection from Pike County. Armitstead's negatives were discovered with the records of the Gulf Mobile, and Ohio Railroad, for whom he worked in the late nineteenth century. His pictures document the region's social and economic activity. Barnett, a Methodist minister in China Grove and an amateur photographer, left few yet fascinating pictures of rural blacks. His negatives were found almost by chance in an old building.

Alabama is fortunate also to have a number of print collections in depositories throughout the state. However, most of these consist of recently made copy prints, generally of poor quality. Many prints are in more than one collection, and the original negatives cannot be found. Some print collections are kept in manila folders, others are sleeved in photograph albums that are stored on shelves. Most contain a mixture of copy and original prints, post cards, and newspaper clippings. Several institutions have attempted to put their holdings in some order, but most collections are poorly catalogued and stored under conditions so inadequate as to threaten their preservation.

The Alabama State Department of Archives and History in Montgomery houses the largest print collection. It covers most aspects of life in Alabama during the New South era with special emphasis on Montgomery and the state's leading political figures. A model for local archives, the Birmingham Public Library has an extensive collection of prints relating to the "Magic City." Efforts to improve housing and cataloguing of this collection have been enhanced by recent acquisitions. The collection provides numerous photographs that enlarge our understanding of the early social and economic history of the state's largest and one of the South's most important industrial centers. In conjunction with the Knox Collection, the Birmingham Public Library holdings enable a researcher to gain a better understanding of that city's turbulent beginnings.

The public libraries of Huntsville and Dothan also have collections of value. Unfortunately, both collections are composed of recent prints made from copy negatives, and some are of poor quality. However, they do contain material on the development of two major sections of the state, the Tennessee River valley and the agricultural area of the southeast known as the "wiregrass" region.

The large print holdings of the Museum of the City of Mobile have been reorganized in recent years and are valuable. Like Birmingham, Mobile has a well-documented past when negative and print collections are considered together. Tuskegee Institute's collection of prints, like Auburn's, documents the history of the school and its region. Various schools and historic societies around the state hold smaller print collections. One of the most notable is the Brantley Collection at Samford University in Birmingham, which includes pictures of small towns in northern Alabama a century ago. Samford is also developing a valuable group of prints, the Harper Collection, which reveals working conditions in early twentieth-century Birmingham. The Ed Leigh McMillan Collection in Brewton, the William P. Reynolds Collection of the Greenville Public Library, the Pike County Pioneer Museum, and the offices of the Fairhope Single Tax Corporation also contain useful collections of prints, though the material in each is primarily of local interest. Most of the major negative collections also have print files.

Photographs of value relating to Alabama also exist outside the state, particularly in the Lewis Hine Collection in the library of the University of Maryland at Baltimore County. Hine made several trips to Alabama as a photographer for the National Child Labor Committee, and many of his prints are famous. His work, coupled with similar pictures taken by local photographers, remind us of how hard life in the New South could be for its people. Other Alabama photographs are contained in the collections of the National Archives, most of which were taken by official government photographers and record the role of the federal government in the construction of dams and locks along the state's inland waterways.

While the major collections of negatives and prints are better cared for today than they were a decade ago, most fall short of the standards of excellence their curators would like to maintain. Preservation is expensive, and the accumulated neglect of previous decades has added to the cost. Some small collections are well maintained, but most are relegated to out-of-the-way shelves and filing cabinets. Few are catalogued, indexed, or stored in a manner acceptable to most archives. There are probably many private collections of negatives and prints whose condition is worse still. It is hoped that many of these will be made available to major archives where they can be cared for, catalogued, and preserved.

The photographic collections in Alabama and those in other states represent an immensely rich historical source. Until recently historians, trained in the use of written sources, have paid them scant attention. Yet photographs can make extremely valuable contributions to our understanding of the recent past, especially in the areas of economic and social history. The images in this book represent the best surviving work of the photographers of Alabama in the New South era. They convey that time to us in ways words alone cannot manage. To look at them is to see what it was like to live and work in the "Heart of Dixie" nearly a century ago. They provide graphic testimony to the era and its people.

Inasmuch as this work treats only the economic and social life of the state, portraits of political leaders, although readily available, were excluded. So, too, were the formal studio portraits that form the majority of most collections. The photographs selected were chosen for their value as historical documents and their aesthetic quality, and every effort was made to employ candid shots. Photographs illustrating the state's economic development are presented first, dealing in succession with the topics of agriculture, transitional industries, heavy industries, transportation, and urbanization. Photographs of the society that the economic structure supported begin with images of the family itself and move to other aspects of social life, including recreation, religion, education, and race relations.

Most of the photographs in this book were made from original negatives or from copy negatives that were made in turn from original prints. In a few cases copy negatives were made from modern copy prints, where no original could be found. Retouched materials were avoided, as their truthfulness is questionable. For this reason no reproductions were made from post cards, the printed page, or engravings. Whenever possible the authors did their own photographic work to be certain of maintaining high technical and academic standards. However, in a few cases this was not possible and prints or copy negatives were supplied by the University of Maryland at Baltimore County, the Auburn University Archives, The University of Alabama in Birmingham's Center for Urban Affairs, the Birmingham Public Library, and the National Archives.

Erik Overbey, Mobile photographer,
1914. (Overbey/Mobile Public Library,
USA Photo Archives)

Pike County man with gun, c. 1915. (Pike
County Collection, USA Photo Archives)

Pike County women, c. 1915. (Pike County Collection, USA Photo Archives)

Mobile women in Mardi Gras ball gowns, c. 1900. (Overbey/Mobile Public Library, USA Photo Archives)

Tuskegee rider, c. 1900. (Tuskegee Institute)

White women, c. 1900. (Overbey/Mobile Public Library, USA Photo Archives)

Rural black woman, Macon County, c. 1900. (Tuskegee Institute)

Pike County family, c. 1915. (Pike County Collection, USA Photo Archives)

Joseph Wheeler and family, c. 1905. Wheeler was an ex-Confederate general, Alabama congressman, and general in the United States Army during the Spanish-American War. (Alabama State Department of Archives and History)

Boy with fish, c. 1895. (Armitstead/Mo-
bile Museum, USA Photo Archives)

The Image of Progress

ALABAMA PHOTOGRAPHS, 1872–1917

Introduction

Because of their depth and variety, the collections of the work of Alabama's early photographers present a unique opportunity to expand our knowledge of the entire post-Reconstruction South, for no state is more representative of the original "New South" than is Alabama. Promoted by a generation of editors, industrialists, and businessmen, the New South was a response both to the defeat of the Old and to the harsh economic realities of the time. Its proponents throughout the region marshaled the energies of a predominately rural and agricultural society in an attempt to create an urban and industrial economy. Coal and iron ore deposits in the Birmingham area provided the foundation for the South's largest mining industry and only major iron and steel center. In Alabama's pine and cypress forests, as in those of other Southern states, lumbering was transformed from a loosely organized, preindustrial activity into a highly mechanized and organized modern industry. Textile mills, the symbol of the new industrial South, sprang up in cities and larger towns and along the upper stretches of the Chattahoochee River valley. Rail systems were expanded or created to serve the state's growing industries, and the improved rail systems in turn encouraged further industrialization.

Alabama's efforts to join the heralded New South were prompted by a new element in the state's political leadership. As elsewhere in the South, this new political faction was composed of industrialists, railroad entrepreneurs, urban merchants, and newspaper editors. They were determined to build an industrial economy modeled after that of the Northern foe that the Civil War had shown so superior. Alabama would enlarge her railroads, expand her commerce, and build her cities; in short, Alabama would have "progress." But advocates of the New South did not desire progress for its own sake. Instead they saw industrialization as a means to achieve economic independence and to end the region's longstanding colonial relationship with the North. They also believed that an industrialized New South could retain much of the informal, personal style of the Old, and thus prove superior to Northern society, which Southerners viewed as cold, impersonal, and materialistic. Because they held such assumptions, proponents of the New South saw no irony in attempting to justify their vision of an industrial society by appealing to the values of an agrarian past.

The advocates of the New South were not without their detractors, however. The planter class, which had dominated Alabama politics prior to the Civil War, emerged from Reconstruction as a still powerful faction. They fought to maintain their traditionally privileged status and to ensure their control over the recently freed black labor force. Although they could support the New South programs that posed no threat to them or that promised to enhance their economic position, such as the extension of rail services or the construction of cotton mills, planters opposed industrial development that threatened their labor supply or their status as the state's dominant economic interest. Outside the plantation region the state's rural residents were small farmers who clung to the Jeffersonian ideal of the yeoman farmer. While not opposed to industrial development, they sought legislation that would make the small farmer the dominant factor in a more diversified agricultural economy. Within this swirl of clashing economic and class interests, the state's black citizens struggled to improve their economic and social status. But the demands of industrialists, planters, and farmers alike for their labor at the lowest possible price, their lack of political power, and the strength of racial prejudice combined to make the blacks' struggle a futile one.

For those who dreamed of a new industrial society, the realities of Alabama's postwar economy posed major problems. Agriculture continued to dominate the state's economy and cotton remained the major crop. Rural residents made up more than 80 percent of the state's total population throughout the New South era. But within this seemingly static agrarian society fundamental changes were occurring. Despite calls for agricultural diversification from both small farmers and New South advocates, the state became increasingly dependent on cotton production. The independent subsistence farmer practically ceased to exist as economic forces bound ever larger numbers of farmers to the cotton culture. The shrinking size of the average farm, down from 222 acres in 1870 to 78.9 acres in 1910, reflected another ominous change, the rapid growth of farm tenancy. In 1880, 53 percent of Alabama's farmers owned their farms; by 1910 that figure had dropped to 39 percent.

As in the rest of the South the rapid increase in farm tenancy and growing dependency on cotton had racial overtones, but neither trend affected solely the black farmer. Thousands of white farmers lost their land, some becoming tenants on the farms they and their families had owned for generations. The percentage of white tenants climbed steadily and by the 1920s whites composed a majority of the tenant population. But because blacks had not obtained land as a result of Reconstruction and because they had fewer economic alternatives than did whites, throughout the New South era a much higher percentage of all blacks were tenants. While black landowners were not rare, they were few. In 1910, nearly a half century after emancipation, only 15 percent of Alabama's blacks owned the farms they operated.

Alabama's tenant system was typical of that of the other Southern states. It rested upon an elaborate complex of crop lien and mortgage laws that granted ultimate control of both farm and tenant to the planter or merchant. The system evolved as a response to the region's lack of capital and its need for agricultural labor. The collapse of the Confederacy depleted the capital reserves of the South, a capital-poor society even before the Civil War. The loss of capital forced the region to turn to tenancy, and, once established, the system proved self-perpetuating. Southern bankers loaned borrowed Northern capital to country merchants and landholders. Merchants and planters in turn advanced funds and supplies to tenants and secured their advances by requiring tenants to plant cotton. This rigid credit system insured the overproduction of cotton, which resulted in chronically depressed cotton prices. It also sent a steady flow of Southern capital in the form of interest to the Northeast, and thus slowed capital accumulation in the South. Similar forces caused other Southern states to adopt a cotton economy as essentially colonial in nature as that of Alabama. During the New South era, Alabama's cotton production increased steadily; the 1910 crop surpassed the bumper crop of 1860 by more than 100,000 bales. Yet in the same period Alabama's share of the nation's total cotton crop declined. This statistic

reveals both the dramatic effect of the crop lien system on cotton production throughout the South and the continued expansion of the cotton culture into the states of the Southwest. It also indicates the intractable nature of the economic problems of Alabama and the South.

Agricultural statistics alone fail to convey the bleak realities of tenant farm life. Farming proved stubbornly resistant to mechanization and required tremendous expenditures of human energy. Farmers still cleared land with axe and hoe and guided mule-drawn plows to break the soil. Hoe gangs, often made up of women and children, still cultivated row crops under an unrelenting summer sun. Workers continued to harvest by hand the major crops of cotton and corn. The hours of labor were not reduced from those of the antebellum period; sunup to sundown remained the standard workday. At periods of peak activity—especially planting, early cultivation, and the harvest—farm laborers worked at a frantic pace the entire day. During slack periods, while a farmer might take time to hunt or fish, the tasks of routine maintenance were never completed.

Alabama's farmers received little reward for their labor. By denying them a choice of what to plant and forcing them to pay exorbitant interest on supplies, the crop lien system doomed to failure their efforts to extricate themselves from their economic plight. Caught in the scissors of declining cotton prices and increasing prices of consumer items and agricultural supplies, the tenant was fortunate if at the year's end he were not further in debt to the landlord; the small farmer was fortunate if he had escaped slipping into tenancy. As the years passed, farmers realized that their economic position was deteriorating. Through no fault of their own they found themselves trapped in a life of poverty that could lead only to resignation and despair or some form of revolt.

Proponents of industrialization saw in the plight of the poor white farmer a compelling argument for their economic program. The factories and mills they envisioned, some contended, would provide economic alternatives for the family trapped in the tenant system. While others acted from less altruistic motives, they nevertheless recognized the need for a dependable labor supply if the vast potential of the state's natural resources was to be developed.

They were determined to forge these resources and the state's indigenous population into the foundation of an industrial economy. To some extent, they succeeded. Ironically, however, Alabama's new industries developed the same colonial relationship with the Northeast that was characteristic of her agricultural economy.

The timber industry early demonstrated the pattern of industrial colonial dependence, both in Alabama and in the seaboard region of other Southern states. In many respects an extension of the agrarian economy, the timber industry utilized an abundant natural resource and could be run with unskilled labor. But large tracts of timberland, modern logging equipment, and sawmilling machinery were expensive, so Northern and foreign capital quickly came to dominate the industry. By the turn of the century huge lumber companies employed thousands of laborers, both white and black, who cut the state's timber stands at an unprecedented rate; and the value of timber exported through Mobile surpassed that of cotton. Alabama's timber exports, however, followed the old trade patterns. Native entrepreneurs paid high interest rates for Northern capital which they used to finance the extraction of a natural resource that was shipped to the North or to Europe. In a truly colonial relationship, Alabama allowed others to manufacture finished products from the natural resources she supplied.

More than any other, the textile industry was financed by native capital, and Southern entrepreneurs controlled the industry throughout the New South era. Textiles played an important role in the industrialization of Alabama, although the state had fewer mills than did the Carolinas and Georgia. The industry was concentrated in the upper Chattahoochee River valley along the Georgia border and in major urban areas. Yet, as in other Southern states, Alabama's fledgling textile industry exhibited several characteristics of industries in colonial economies. Mills in which women and children were not a majority of the work force were few, and in many they were at least three-fourths of all employees. Supervisory personnel and highly skilled laborers were frequently imported from New England textile centers, especially in the years prior to 1900. The modern spinning and weaving machinery installed in the Southern mills was also purchased from New

England firms. Because of a lack of skilled labor and other economic factors, Alabama's mills produced coarse yarns and inexpensive fabrics. The cloth from her mills was shipped North to be manufactured into finished garments.

Not even the wealth of the Birmingham area's deposits of coal, iron ore, and limestone could break the traditional economic patterns, although this mineral triad assured the development of a major iron and steel industry. Both native and Northern capitalists invested in the region during the 1870s and early 1880s. The most significant investors, however, were the Tennessee Coal and Iron Company and the Louisville and Nashville Railroad, both of which brought large sums of Northern capital into the Birmingham region. Outside capital became increasingly dominant in the last decade of the nineteenth century. In 1907, J. P. Morgan's United States Steel Company acquired the Tennessee Coal and Iron Company, thus making the Birmingham iron and steel complex essentially an extension of the Pittsburgh giant. Whatever her dreams of sectional economic independence through industrialization, Alabama saw her major new industry assume the old colonial dependence on Northern capital.

The story was the same in the railroad industry. Two lines came to dominate the industry, the Alabama Great Southern, which after the panic of 1893 absorbed several smaller lines to create the Southern Railway, and the Louisville and Nashville. The latter controlled access to the state's mineral region and was itself a major investor in the coal and iron industries. Hence the Louisville and Nashville became the most powerful political force in the state, a position it maintained until the end of the New South era. The nineteenth century witnessed a rapid growth of track mileage and the consolidation of smaller lines. Alabama's railroads adopted the standard gauge in 1886, thus achieving integration into the national rail system. Northern capital financed most of these developments, as it did in other Southern states. Well before 1900, Northern financial interests controlled Alabama's railroads, again emphasizing the colonial nature of the state's economy.

While the state's developing industries fell into the old colonial patterns, their development nevertheless created changes within Alabama's economy. Improved rail facilities, for example, reduced

the shipment of cotton on the state's extensive river systems, causing the economy of Mobile, the state's only seaport, to languish. The lack of a water route between Mobile and the industrial region around Birmingham hampered the development of both cities. Not until 1915 did the completion of a series of locks on the Tombigbee and Black Warrior rivers make water transportation between the state's two major cities possible. These facilities, used by barges and tugs, brought to an end the era of the old river steamer that had been the mainstay of the antebellum river traffic.

By the end of the era the automobile had begun to alter transportation patterns, although its full impact would be felt only after World War I. Within the city the automobile's influence upon economic and social activities was immediate and profound. It began to replace the team and wagon as the means of transporting goods within urban areas and created support industries such as garages and service stations. The automobile quickened the expansion of the cities into suburban areas, and the "Sunday drive" provided a new leisure activity. With the spread of the automobile into rural areas, the public demanded road-building programs of their elected officials, thus spurring the development of yet another related industry.

The years 1880-1910 witnessed a threefold increase in Alabama's urban population, an increase prompted by a chronically depressed agricultural economy, the opportunities for migration provided by improved transportation facilities, and the lure of industrial employment. As elsewhere in the South, the city enticed the more venturesome of the disenchanted rural residents with its promise of economic opportunity and an escape from the drudgery of farm life. The absence of formal apprenticeship systems encouraged farm boys possessing the most rudimentary skills to move to the city and become members of a number of trades. Others became clerks, stevedores, teamsters, and manual laborers. Women entered the work force as both clerical and industrial workers. A variety of urban firms offered employment to the children of migrating farm families.

The most rapid urban growth occurred in the mineral belt of north Alabama and reflected the development of the iron and coal industries. Founded in 1871, Birmingham symbolized the dynamic

growth of the entire New South. By 1900 the population of the "Magic City" surpassed 38,000, and within another decade it had grown to 132,685 persons and was one of the largest cities in the South. Other towns spawned by the coal and iron booms of the 1870s and 1880s included Gadsden, Anniston, Bessemer, and Ensley.

Urban growth outside the mineral region, though less dramatic, was steady. Mobile remained the state's largest city until 1890, even though the Civil War had disrupted its cotton trade. By the 1890s lumber and coal had supplemented its declining cotton exports and stimulated an economic revival. Although outstripped by Birmingham, in 1910 Mobile had a population of over 50,000 people. In Montgomery, state government, railroads, and agriculture sustained three decades of growth, and by 1910 that city had over 38,000 residents. In the Tennessee River valley Huntsville remained the most important commercial center, while Dothan occupied a similar position in the newer agricultural counties of the southeastern "wiregrass" region.

Despite significant gains, however, Alabama's urban population continued to lag behind that of the nation or of the South. Alabama's rate of urban growth was high, exceeded only by that of Mississippi and North Carolina, but the rate of growth reflected the extremely rural nature of all three states in 1880. By 1910, Texas, Louisiana, Virginia, Tennessee, Georgia, and Florida all had higher percentages of urban population than did Alabama, and all but Florida had a greater number of urban residents. Nationally, 42 percent of the population resided in urban areas by 1910, a figure two and one-half times greater than Alabama's urban population. In urbanization, as in industrialization, Alabama and the South found that tremendous advancement within the state or region was offset by even greater advances in the more industrialized states of the North.

Nevertheless, at the turn of the century Alabama's cities reflected the changes that New South advocates sought. Birmingham, symbol of industrialization, had replaced Mobile, the antebellum cotton port, as the state's largest, most vital city. In the state's major urban centers, a working class was taking shape. More significantly, a well-defined urban middle class had emerged and was making its presence felt in state politics. Without abandoning its goal of industrial progress, the middle class joined the working class in demanding reform of some of the severe social problems that resulted from urbanization and industrialization. Simultaneously, the sheer number of people in the cities created a variety of cultural and social activities that surpassed by far those found in antebellum Alabama outside Mobile.

Yet another change prompted by postwar economic development was the creation of a new work force. While this new labor force grew most rapidly in urban areas, its expansion was not limited to the city. Many Alabama industries, like those in other Southern states, were located in rural areas. Mining villages and lumber camps, for example, developed in rural areas, as did many cotton mills. By World War I, a sizable nonagrarian labor force had emerged, although a number of social and economic factors limited its influence.

With few exceptions, Alabama's nonagrarian labor force resembled that of the other Southern states and was typical of a labor force in colonial economies. Native labor, recruited from the farms and villages of the Alabama countryside, filled its ranks. Recruiting posed no problem, for labor was plentiful. Everywhere men and women, black and white, sought industrial jobs in an effort to escape the poverty and isolation of the farm. To the tenant farmer, the most menial industrial employment offered hope of a comparatively high standard of living. As a result, thousands of rural Alabamians vied for the relatively few industrial positions. Urban textile mill owners, lumber mill barons in the pine belt, and blast furnace operators and mine owners in the mineral region all enjoyed a surplus of labor.

While this pool of surplus native labor practically eliminated the need for immigrants, some foreign-born and non-Southern workers joined the work force, especially in the Birmingham iron and steel industry. As in most colonial economies the local people received the unskilled positions. In the coal fields British miners obtained skilled positions, including the dangerous jobs associated with blasting operations. In the late 1880s mine operators recruited Italian workers to ensure a surplus of manual labor, a practice bitterly resented by native miners. Lack of skilled native labor also caused the textile industry to import mill superintendents and other skilled personnel from New England.

Alabama's labor force was more racially mixed than that of the upper South, a fact that reflected the mining and lumber industries' need for manual labor and the smaller proportion of the state's total labor force employed by the almost exclusively white textile industry. Blacks made up 46 percent of the state's coal miners in 1889, a figure slightly higher than the percentage of blacks in the total population. Blacks also labored in the mineral region's quarries, blast furnaces, foundries, and steel and iron mills. Within these industries, however, traditional racial patterns were observed: whites held the skilled positions and blacks worked for the most part as manual laborers. In the woods, loggers worked in segregated gangs and lived in segregated camps. Urban blacks worked as stevedores, as teamsters, in the construction trades, and in some service occupations. But the depression of 1893 intensified urban white opposition to black economic advancement and contributed to the development of legal segregation and disenfranchisement at the turn of the century. Driven from skilled positions in the trades, blacks were relegated to domestic service and manual labor, which at best paid survival wages.

As in the upper South, blacks were practically excluded from Alabama's textile industry. They rarely worked inside the mills and never as operators of machinery. The exclusion of blacks from the textile industry underscored the powerful sexual implications of racial segregation, for of the New South industries, the textile mills relied most heavily on white female workers. Whites refused to tolerate blacks working in close proximity to white women and children in an industrial setting where the mores of an agrarian society might be questioned. Other Alabama industries employed an almost exclusively male labor force. Because women were not present and blacks were either kept segregated or employed in inferior positions, whites did not regard the hiring of blacks by these industries as a major threat to the South's racial code.

Like members of the emerging nonagrarian labor force throughout the South, Alabama's laborers encountered grim working conditions and could do little to effect reform. Their efforts were hampered by a lack of economic alternatives, a surplus labor pool, and racial prejudice as well as their lack of education and organization. The political power of the industrialists and the laissez faire sentiments of the era isolated the laborer from other elements of society and worked against the creation of a public demand for reform. Throughout the era Alabama workers received wages considerably lower than those paid Northern laborers. Many firms paid laborers in scrip redeemable only at company stores, often at less than face value for overpriced goods. Alabama workers also labored longer hours than did their Northern counterparts. For all practical purposes working hours were unrestricted and varied from ten to twelve hours in the mines to twelve and fourteen hours in lumber and textile mills. Progressive legislation passed after the turn of the century to restrict the working hours of women and children was generally ineffective and rarely enforced.

Laborers faced other equally flagrant abuses, all of which were commonly employed by firms in other Southern states. Exploitation of child labor was a standard practice in textile mills, although that industry was not the sole offender. Coal mines employed boys, and urban businesses employed both boys and girls in a variety of positions. The convict lease system provided mine operators with a supply of cheap, predominately black labor that could also be used to break strikes. Despite protests from free labor and humanitarians, conservative state legislatures refused to alter a system that returned monies to the state while benefiting its most influential industries. By 1894 nearly 1,400 convicts were laboring in the state's coal mines. The company town, present in the textile, mining, lumber, and iron and steel industries, presented management with another means of controlling the workers.

The abuses of the young industries did not go completely unchallenged, and by the end of the era several factors had combined to persuade industrialists to abandon some of their most exploitative practices. The late 1880s and early 1890s saw miners strike in opposition to the convict lease system and for higher wages. By the turn of the century, reformers joined the miners in their demands for the abolition of convict labor, although that goal would be achieved only after World War I. An Episcopal priest from Montgomery, Edgar Garner Murphy, led progressives and urban factory workers in a protracted and moderately successful

campaign to restrict the employment of children. Industrialists began to realize that "social welfare" programs for laborers could increase both productivity and employee loyalty. After the panic of 1907 precipitated a major miners' strike against the Tennessee Coal and Iron Company in 1908, the company took the lead in establishing educational, recreational, and health programs for its employees. Other industries followed suit, frequently providing services superior to those provided by state or local governments.

The changes that occurred in Alabama's economy from Reconstruction to World War I, with few exceptions, followed the general pattern of development in the remainder of the South. The state constructed water and rail transportation systems that have changed little since that era. A small but expanding industrial sector was established as were urban growth patterns that would continue until World War II. An increasingly powerful faction of the state's political leadership remained convinced of the need for further industrialization. These changes, however, did not fundamentally alter the society. Agriculture remained the dominant economic activity and Alabama remained an overwhelmingly rural state, with over 80 percent of its people residing in rural areas. Even among the urban residents, many of whom had recently left the farm, rural social and cultural values prevailed. Most significantly, economic development during the era failed to break the state's colonial relationship with the North, and in some cases economic dependence was strengthened. With its sister Southern states, Alabama remained outside the mainstream of the national economy.

Despite the efforts of New South advocates of industrialization and rapid economic development, the people of Alabama and the South clung to the social and cultural values of the antebellum era. Even those who urged industrialization were not prepared to abandon the values of the past. Rather, the late nineteenth-century South sought to adopt the economic system of the victorious North for the same reason modern developing nations have attempted to duplicate the economies of former colonial powers—to achieve economic independence. The South also associated economic independence with political independence, just as modern developing nations have linked economic and political goals. The

South, however, rather than seeking the independence of national sovereignty, which it had lost on the battlefields of the Civil War, sought political independence within the federal system. Just as recently formed nation-states have rejected the culture of former Western colonial powers, the post-Civil War South rejected much of the culture of the dominant North and attempted to preserve Southern traditional values. In *The Mind of the South*, Wilbur J. Cash observed that in none of the South's acceptance of industrialization "was there any realization that the abandonment of the purely agricultural way and the fetching in of the machine would call for the remolding of the old purely agricultural mind." Paul Gaston, a more recent scholar, wrote in *The New South Creed* that spokesmen for the New South "understood instinctively that no program of reform could do violence to a universally cherished past and hope to succeed."

Promoting rapid economic development through industrialization while simultaneously attempting to maintain existing social and cultural values is a common pattern among "developing" nations. As an agricultural society undergoing the initial stages of industrialization, one that remained in a colonial relationship with the economically and militarily stronger North, the post-Civil War South fit this pattern. Among modern developing nations, some have proved more adept than others at maintaining traditional values. In Alabama and the South during the postwar era, a number of factors combined to make the state and the region remarkably resistant to social and cultural change.

The normal human reluctance to relinquish a familiar life-style accounts for much of Alabama's resistance to social change. But Southerners clung to their traditional values for more compelling reasons, the most important being their genuine fondness for and appreciation of them. The absence of a "modern" industrial economy did not, after all, prevent the antebellum South from creating a deeply satisfying, appealing life-style, not just among the plantation elite, but for the entire white population. As recent scholarship has demonstrated, even the slave community developed its own unique folkways that, within the restraints of the system, met the slaves' social and cultural needs. Southern society, for example, was based on a powerful, almost clannish, family structure. For

urban and rural residents social life revolved about the family. Visits by distant relatives broke the daily routine for both guests and hosts and strengthened family ties. The family picnic was a favorite recreational activity among all classes. The family reunion, an extremely popular event among rural folk, was retained by those who migrated to the cities. Held annually, reunions often attracted hundreds of relatives both from within and without the state for a day of feasting, singing, and honoring family bonds. In many respects, Southern culture was fundamentally a tightly interwoven system of family relationships.

The church, too, was a powerful force in the social life of most Alabamians. In addition to its primary religious function, the Sunday worship service provided an opportunity for neighbors to visit and, especially in rural areas, furthered an exchange of information on topics as varied as the condition of crops, the health of local residents, and local political activity. Although Protestant churches discouraged the use of alcohol, dancing, gambling, and other social activities considered immoral, they compensated by providing entertainment and social events both for their members and for the people of the larger community. Begun in rural areas but retained by urban churches, the "revival" or camp meeting was one of the most important events of the year. Revivals, usually held for a week each summer, attracted crowds who came to visit friends and family, to be entertained by hymn singing and the preacher's oratory, and to worship. Like many other church activities, revivals played a prominent role in the "courting" patterns of the young. Church picnics and homecomings attracted large crowds and week-night prayer meetings interrupted the monotony of the workweek. Among the Baptists and several other denominations, baptism was both a social and religious event. Crowds "gathered at the river" to rejoice as the immersed convert emerged a member of the faithful.

Civic and fraternal organizations lent variety to Alabama's social life. In small towns they frequently occupied the largest building other than a church or school. Such organizations prospered primarily because of their social role, but they served other purposes. Usually segregated by sex, they reinforced the narrowly defined sex roles of the era. Masons, Red Men, Woodmen of the World, and other groups created forums in which the community's male leadership discussed the social, economic, and political events of the day. Women's clubs, often concerned with the development of domestic skills, provided one of the few approved recreational activities for women. During the Progressive movement, however, the clubs also gave women a platform from which to demand social reforms and a role in politics. They also offered one of the few opportunities for women to develop leadership skills.

Perhaps nothing better reveals the ability of the people of the New South to bring joy and meaning to their lives than the music of the region. While the other arts fared poorly because of generally low income and educational levels, among the common folk music flourished. Hand-held, relatively inexpensive instruments such as the fiddle, banjo, mandolin, guitar, and harmonica provided accompaniment for singing and dancing. The more prosperous gathered about the family piano or organ to sing their favorite hymns and secular tunes. In urban and rural areas, young ladies of the middle class were expected to study either the piano or the violin. Towns organized marching bands whose martial music, often more exuberant than accomplished, signaled a spirit of civic pride. Churches promoted musical education by means as divergent as the a cappella Sacred Harp singing of some fundamentalist denominations to the Bach organ preludes of large urban churches.

Like most Southerners, the people of Alabama loved outdoor sports. Hunting and fishing were the most popular, and there were few rural residents who did not enjoy one or the other. Because towns were small and well within walking distance of field and stream, many urban residents also participated in both sports. Many wealthy hunters rode to the hounds while the average man stalked small game. In cities and towns organized sports, especially baseball and football, captured the interests of spectators as well as participants. With few exceptions, organized sports were the males' domain. In a few urban areas girls' basketball teams could be found. Elsewhere young girls might take part in childhood games, fishing, and bathing, provided proper decorum was observed. Otherwise young ladies were expected to engage in the less strenuous "domestic arts."

A variety of other events woven into the fabric of the social life of the common folk interrupted the tedium of daily routine with a special type of excitement. The excursion was among the most popular of such events. Residents of city, town, and village set out on excursions by train or less frequently by boat. The Gulf of Mexico and Mobile Bay and the mountains of north Alabama were favorite excursion destinations, and by the turn of the century resorts in both areas catered to the tourist trade. An occasional circus or carnival, traveling medicine shows, and the annual fall agricultural fairs that were held in many counties and on a regional and state level increased the frequency, if not the quality, of the entertainment available to Alabamians. Nothing, however, could match the sheer excitement generated by a political canvass. A heritage of the antebellum period, a good, emotional, political canvass featuring two or more popular orators attracted enthusiastic crowds in rural and urban areas.

Considered together, the more attractive aspects of life in Alabama during the New South era underscored the ability of its people to derive pleasure from simple activities. In a society so economically poor, it could hardly have been otherwise. At one level, the enjoyment of simple pleasures made the best of life under bleak economic conditions. Yet on another level such pleasures gave life meaning, even a richness. It was to these qualities of their life-style that Alabamians were genuinely attached and of which they were justifiably proud. Seen from a different perspective, however, the pleasurable aspects of life only served to make harsh economic realities endurable; pleasant pastimes could not alter economic facts. The warmth of a family reunion, the excitement of a revival, or the thrill of the hunt gave Alabamians a sense of belonging, a concept of individual worth, a means of momentarily escaping economic demands. But such activities could not obscure the economic and social plight of the majority of the state's citizens, or the fact that their plight contributed to the state's resistance to change.

Without question, poverty was the greatest single factor influencing resistance to social and cultural change. Poverty was the common denominator in the lives of most Alabamians, whether they worked on the farm or in the factory. Its hold on the society was longstanding. The penury of the antebellum agrarian economy and the devastation of war placed Alabamians under enormous economic burdens. A chronically depressed postwar agricultural economy tightened poverty's grip on the state and region. It dictated the life-styles of most Alabamians and hampered the development of institutions that could have enriched their lives. Poverty retarded the growth of educational systems, choked artistic and cultural development, and left the state's citizenry easy prey for the political demagogue.

Racial prejudice, another antebellum legacy, helped buttress the values of the past. Neither the war nor Reconstruction had shaken the white population's belief in the inferiority of blacks and their determination to see that the South remained a "white man's country." Given this basic reality, the collapse of Reconstruction threw race relations into a state of uncertainty and initiated an extended period of racial conflict. Whites sought once again to subordinate blacks, who struggled to retain what they could of the gains of the Reconstruction era. Out of this bitter and sometimes violent struggle emerged the strident segregationist attitudes that would characterize Alabama and the South until the 1970s.

A strongly held, if somewhat distorted, view of the past slowed the deterioration of traditional values. The shared experience of defeat and military occupation created a common bond among Southern whites, causing them to glorify the society they had defended and their defense of it. In so doing they created a usable view of the past that rested upon two concepts. The first was the myth of a gracious, benevolent planter society. The second was the "Lost Cause" of the Confederacy. Like other Southerners, Alabamians created numerous social, fraternal, and military organizations through which they expressed their devotion to the ideals of the Confederacy and honored the courage of those who had defended it. Such organizations and activities fostered a preoccupation with antebellum values and questioned those of the Northern foe.

Their desire for economic progress was not the sole aspiration that conflicted with the natural desire of the people of Alabama and the South to retain their traditional values. Though devoted to the ideals of the Confederacy, Alabamians longed to rejoin the national mainstream and to find acceptance as Americans. But they sought to do so on their own terms while maintaining a separate identity. At the same time they desired to be viewed as equals within the American family. Throughout the New South era Alabamians believed, with some justification, that the rest of the nation saw Southerners as prodigals, chastized but not forgiven. Southerners, on the other hand, expected the North to extend a biblical welcome to the prodigals, without requiring them to acknowledge their waywardness. Compounding the problem was the Southerners' sense of inferiority, heightened by defeat, which led them to cling even more tenaciously to an idealized past while seeking full partnership in America's present and future. This desire to be accepted as equals, yet to retain a separate identity, also follows a pattern discernible among emerging societies of the post-World War II era.

In the long run, economic and social realities thwarted the South's goal of acceptance more than did the region's insistence on retaining traditional values or the North's reluctance to welcome an unrepentant South. In some respects, Alabama and the South became less like the North during the New South period, thus making their acceptance as equals less likely. During the era, for example, the "New Immigrants" of southern and eastern Europe transformed the ethnic composition of the population of the North and Midwest. Few immigrants, however, came South. In Alabama, Birmingham and its surrounding mineral belt proved the major exception to this rule. There Welsh and Italian miners, small Jewish and Greek communities, and native Southerners of both races made up one of the most ethnically diverse populations to be found in the South. Birmingham owed its ethnic diversity not only to its mineral wealth, but to its youth as well. Developed entirely after the war, Birmingham and its sister cities of the mineral region were more attractive to immigrants in part because of their lack of antebellum tradition.

Outside the Birmingham area the white population remained overwhelmingly British in origin and Protestant by persuasion. Within this relatively homogeneous society, most Protestant denominations preached an emotionally charged evangelical fundamentalism, giving their Christianity a distinctly Old Testament flavor. The Bible represented the literal truth, heaven and hell were as real as Birmingham and Mobile, and religion consisted of efforts to enter the one and avoid the other. Yet Southern churches were not completely untouched by developments outside the region. By the turn of the century the social gospel, despite stiff resistance from some church members, had begun to influence some of the urban churches of the mainline denominations. Nor was Protestantism universal. In Birmingham, Mobile, and Montgomery, Judaism and Catholicism were firmly established. Members of both faiths were accepted by their communities until the rise of the Ku Klux Klan at the end of the era led to outbreaks of anti-Catholicism in the Birmingham area. In the main, however, the rural and small town societies failed to develop a sense of religious and ethnic pluralism that was emerging elsewhere in the nation. Yet especially in these areas, religion comforted Alabamians in time of tragedy, reinforced their social values, and provided them with a means of expressing a sense of individual worth.

While the North forged ahead with the development of public schools that were essential to the process of nationalizing millions of immigrant children, in the South public education languished. Alabama's Bourbon Democrats, seeking to lower taxes, slashed educational budgets and shifted funds from black to white schools. The results of such shortsighted policies were as tragic as they were predictable. Well into the twentieth century the state had only a rudimentary school system for whites, and educational opportunities for blacks were pathetic. State-supported high schools were not established until 1907. At the turn of the century Alabama spent approximately fifty cents per capita for public education, less than a tenth the sum spent by the states of the Northeast. Only 65 percent of the eligible school population attended classes, and the school term ran less than seventy days. Nearly 15 percent of the white population and almost half of the black population were illiterate. Although the Progressive era witnessed substantial improvements in the state's schools, at the end of the New South era Alabama still lacked an effective educational system for whites, and blacks were fortunate to receive even the most rudimentary education.

In its bid for national acceptance the South continued to be hampered by its most enduring problem—the race issue. Increasingly after 1876, the racial issue became the "Southern question" as the North turned its back on the problem. In Alabama and the South race relations deteriorated steadily, reaching their nadir at the turn of the century. Whites cut funding for black schools to a pittance, segregated transportation facilities, forbade blacks to frequent public accommodations used by whites, and framed laws that fell most heavily upon blacks and sent thousands into the convict labor system. Violence threatened any black who protested such treatment, and hundreds of blacks were lynched during the era. Like other Southern states, at the turn of the century Alabama disenfranchised its black citizens to ensure white control over the society. Disenfranchisement, racial violence, and harsh segregation legislation placed a moral onus upon Alabama and the South, although Northern racial attitudes and policies were hardly enlightened and the federal government had adopted racial segregation as an official policy by the end of the era.

Other factors hampered Alabamians in their efforts to obtain equality within the national society. The agrarian population's continued dominance over the state's relatively small urban community isolated Alabama from the social and cultural developments of the North. Because of rapid industrialization in the North, the farmer was no longer regarded as the respected independent producer, the virtuous pillar of an idealized agrarian state. Rather he became the uneducated hayseed, lacking in sophistication. In a land dedicated to prosperity and self-advancement, he was a symbol of economic depression, social stagnation, even downward social mobility. A poor society with a largely uneducated people, the South lagged behind the North in cultural development. The arts and letters fared badly in Alabama, although a strong folk culture developed among its populace that was especially evident in the vigor and creativity of their music. In higher education, too, Alabama reflected the South's inability to keep pace with the advances of the industrial states of the North and Midwest.

As Southerners, Alabamians were torn between their loyalty to the "Lost Cause" of the Confederacy and their desire to be considered Americans. Their allegiance to traditional values conflicted with their desire for economic change. Such fundamental conflicts resulted in something approaching cultural schizophrenia. Alabamians celebrated the Fourth of July *and* Robert E. Lee's birthday. They could lionize Henry Grady, the Georgian who was the region's leading spokesman for industrialization, and yet extol the virtues of the antebellum planter. Aware of their economic, educational, and cultural shortcomings, they nevertheless viewed themselves and their life-style as the equals of the people and customs of the North. The failure of their effort to create a separate nation, which to Alabamians of the New South was a recent experience rather than a fading memory, reinforced the tendency to view themselves as a people apart. Yet they yearned for acceptance and affirmation of their equality.

In only one area of the national experience during the New South era did the people of Alabama find the acceptance they desired so desperately. War gained for them and other Southerners a measure of equality with their fellow Americans, at least temporarily. War provided Alabamians a link with both the past and the aspirations of the nation. It allowed them to prove their allegiance to the Union they had fought to destroy while at the same time permitted them to celebrate the valor with which they had defended the Confederacy. Their poverty, their educational and cultural deficiencies, even their racial views became, at least for the moment, immaterial. In time of war, their high regard for military courage became a national asset. They could, as Southern Americans, fight for national goals. The Spanish-American War gave them their first opportunity to do so, and Alabamians made the most of it. They welcomed the war and participated in it with pride. With victory and the return of peace, they glorified the exploits of the state's native sons in the conflict. Upon the outbreak of World War I in Europe, they sympathized with the British. Alabamians supported President Wilson's preparedness programs and cheered his decision to go to war. When the war came, many saw in it an opportunity to achieve for both Alabama and the South total acceptance within the national mainstream and a recognition of equality from the remainder of the nation. But they would find that the legacy of racial prejudice, poverty, and their special sense of the past was not so easily shed. They would remain a separate people, still searching for a New South, and with it the solutions to the problems posed by their unique heritage.

The Economic Setting

Because most of the work was done by hand, cotton cultivation required a large labor force. Picking cotton near Huntsville, 1898. (Alabama State Department of Archives and History)

18

PICKER TAKES MIDDLE ROW AND HALF TWO SIDE ROWS.

Early efforts to replace the labor force with machines to cultivate and harvest cotton failed. This unsuccessful steam-driven cotton picker is shown in a field near Montgomery in 1904. (Alabama State Department of Archives and History)

The same merchant or planter who supplied the tenant often owned the only local cotton gin and charged the tenant a ginning fee. Transporting cotton to the gin, Macon County, c. 1900. (Tuskegee Institute)

20

Ginned and baled, cotton was transported by wagon to the nearest local market where it was purchased by buyers representing domestic textile firms, speculators, and others. Wagons in Huntsville's public square, c. 1890. (Auburn University Archives)

Many of the tenants who grew the state's cotton lived in homes such as this one. The plants in the foreground are collards, a nutritious staple of the diet of the rural poor. Macon County, c. 1905. (Tuskegee Institute)

Most farm families, including tenants, cultivated gardens in their "spare time." Gardens produced food that could be stored through winter, such as Irish and sweet potatoes, in addition to seasonal produce. This man tends a "patch of greens," another staple of the diet of the rural poor. Macon County, c. 1900. (Tuskegee Institute)

Clearing land remained one of the hardest tasks in farming. Extracting pine stumps, southern Alabama, c. 1895. (Armitstead/Mobile Museum, USA Photo Archives)

24

Outside the major cotton-producing areas families, white and black, eked out an existence on subsistence farms. Such farms were prevalent in the pine barrens of the south and the hill country of north Alabama. Small farm owners near Kushla in southwestern Alabama, c. 1895. (Armitstead/Mobile Museum, USA Photo Archives)

Some landowners with access to adequate sources of capital experimented with diversified farming, especially in the southern counties where truck farming attracted attention at the turn of the century. Agrarian day laborers in a strawberry field near Castleberry in south Alabama, 1910. (Alabama State Department of Archives and History)

In agriculture as elsewhere, whites received the better jobs, although they were tenants and day laborers. Packing strawberries for shipment, Castleberry, 1910. At right note the supervisor with riding crop, the antebellum overseer's symbol of authority. (Auburn University Archives)

Truck farms raised vegetables for urban markets. Stoop laborers harvest beans, Mobile County. (Wilson Collection, Historic Mobile Preservation Society)

28

Taken at Tuskegee Institute, c. 1900, this photograph illustrates the school's emphasis on "practical agriculture," a concept endorsed by many agrarian reformers. In the lower left of this photograph students care for young chicks. Easy to raise, inexpensive, and tasty, the chicken was a basic protein source in the Southern diet. (Tuskegee Institute)

Small towns served farmers as a market-place and supplied them with seeds, fertilizers, and farm implements. Loading produce at Beaver Meadow, a village in south Alabama, c. 1895. (Armitstead/Mobile Museum, USA Photo Archives)

Even larger communities served primarily as agricultural markets and supply centers. Only Birmingham, the small industrial centers in the mineral region, and to a lesser extent the commercial center of Mobile, escaped the pattern. Florence, 1898. (Alabama State Department of Archives and History)

Merchants and professionals dominated the economic and social life of small towns in Alabama. For those of lesser status small-town life was an experience in economic and cultural poverty as is indicated by this photograph, probably taken to portray the "quaintness" of Southern towns. The town is unidentified in this stereo view, c. 1887. (Alabama State Department of Archives and History)

At the end of the agricultural supply chain was the country store. This typical establishment was near the village of Coden in southern Alabama, c. 1900. (Wilson Collection, Historic Mobile Preservation Society)

Larger agricultural towns represented civilization for farm families of the surrounding countryside. Marion, Alabama, in the heart of the cotton counties of the "Black Belt," 1872. (Brantley Collection, Samford)

34

For such families a trip to the nearest town was a major social event, an interruption of farm life that might occur but once or twice a year. Tuscaloosa, c. 1875. (Brantley Collection, Samford)

Cotton buyers on the streets of the commercial center of the newly settled "wiregrass" counties of southeastern Alabama. Dothan, 1894. (G. S. Houston Library, Dothan)

Because farming remained in a depressed economic state throughout the era, bankruptcy sales of farms and businesses in agricultural towns were not uncommon occurrences. Crowds in Dothan, 1902. (G. S. Houston Library, Dothan)

Prompted by the depressed economy, in the 1890s farmers demanded help from the state and federal government. Their demands resulted in increased appropriations to the Agricultural and Mechanical College at Auburn. Pictured here is a sophomore analytical chemistry class at the Auburn School, 1893. (Auburn University Archives)

Although the Agricultural and Mechanical College at Auburn employed modern techniques on its experimental farms, farmers and tenants adopted reforms slowly. Lack of capital prevented the tractor from threatening the mule; tradition discouraged other modern practices. The A & M College experimental farm, c. 1905. (Auburn University Archives)

Alabama lacked the low country to develop an extensive sugar cane industry, but many farmers in southern counties produced their own cane and syrup. Grinding cane, c. 1895. (Wilson Collection, Historic Mobile Preservation Society)

Essentially an agricultural enterprise, the turpentine industry flourished in the pine belt that stretched from Montgomery to Mobile. Requiring little capital, it was an ideal "transition" industry. A turpentine still in rural south Alabama, c. 1895. (Armitstead/Mobile Museum, USA Photo Archives)

The state's giant pine and cypress forests also supported a major timber industry. In the early days of the postwar industry, logs were hauled for miles on high-wheeled, oxdrawn carts. An early family enterprise, Escambia County, southeast Alabama, c. 1880. (Mills Collection, Brewton)

Like industrial firms in the rest of the nation, lumber companies gave little thought to conservation in their rush to exploit a valuable natural resource. Cutover timberland outside Mobile, c. 1895. (Armitstead/Mobile Museum, USA Photo Archives)

Some timber was floated downriver for export through Mobile. By 1900 the port's timber exports had surpassed in value its exports of cotton. Timber in Mobile harbor, c. 1895. (Armitstead/Mobile Museum, USA Photo Archives)

Throughout the pine belt sawmills sprang up to process the timber felled by logging crews. Sawmilling was an extremely dangerous occupation. Mill hands worked near belts, pulleys, and carriages that moved logs to unguarded blades measuring three and four feet in diameter. A south Alabama mill, c. 1900. (Wilson Collection, Historic Mobile Preservation Society)

Although the cotton mill symbolized the New South, Alabama's textile industry developed somewhat later than that of the upper South and was never so dominant a factor in the state's economy. Nevertheless, the industry was significant, providing an escape from the farm for many white families. Dwarfed by the mill, workers photographed by Lewis Hine return to work at Opelika, 1914. (Bafford Collection, University of Maryland)

In the strictly segregated textile industry, the threat of employing blacks was used to control the white labor force. Few blacks held jobs in the industry, and those who did worked as manual laborers outside the spinning or weaving areas. These youngsters strip the baling from raw cotton. The mill in which they worked, although owned by Mobilians, was just across the state line in Stonewall, Mississippi, c. 1895. (Armitstead/Mobile Museum, USA Photo Archives)

47

As in the rest of the South, the Alabama cotton textile industry relied upon cheap labor, especially that of women and children. Boys in the Barker Cotton Mills, Mobile, 1914. Photograph by Lewis Hine. (Bafford Collection, University of Maryland)

In most spinning mills, girls and young women made up the bulk of the labor force. Girls in the spinning room of Barker Cotton Mills, Mobile, 1914. Photograph by Lewis Hine. (Bafford Collection, University of Maryland)

Alabama's reputation as a leader in the New South was built upon the iron industry that developed from the charcoal furnaces of the antebellum era. Cords of wood and the charcoal ovens at Irontown, near Oxmoor, c. 1880. (Alabama State Department of Archives and History)

Ironton Hotel—Operatives' Houses—Shades' Mountain—S. & N. R.R.—Coal Ovens & Coal-wood-yard
Looking East

Ironworks at Ironton as seen from the Hotel Looking South-of West

Coking coal provided an ingredient essential for the creation of a modern iron industry. Coal cars outside the Bessie Mine near Ensley, 1910. Lewis Hine photograph. (Bafford Collection, University of Maryland)

Iron ore came from the hills surrounding Birmingham. Strip mining at Goethite, near Birmingham, 1911. (University of Alabama)

Mining of both coal and iron ore employed a large labor force, and as elsewhere in the nation relations between miners and their employers were volatile. Miners struck frequently and lost almost as frequently. This photograph shows guards protecting the property of the Tennessee Coal and Iron Company during a major strike in 1894. (From the Collections of the Birmingham Public Library)

54

City convicts in their sleeping quarters. Shackles never removed. July 1907

Wage disputes and the use of convict laborers in the mines prompted most strikes. Both state and county prisoners were used in the mines. Birmingham prisoners, 1907. (Thomas Duke Parke Papers, Department of Archives and Manuscripts, Birmingham Public Library, Birmingham, Alabama)

Despite labor disputes, a lack of capital, and other difficulties, pig iron production increased rapidly and was soon followed by the production of steel. Birmingham's first shipment of steel, 1897. (Center for Urban Affairs, University of Alabama in Birmingham)

FIRST CAR LOAD OF STEEL MADE IN BIRMINGHAM ALA.
JULY 22, 1897.

Because it was new, the steel industry employed the latest technology in the plants of the Birmingham area. Pouring billets at the Tennessee Coal and Iron Company's mill, Birmingham, c. 1900. (Harper Collection, Samford)

As steel production increased, steel fabricating plants sprang up in the area. Pictured here is one such firm, the Henderson Steel and Manufacturing Company, Birmingham, c. 1915. (From the Collections of the Birmingham Public Library)

58

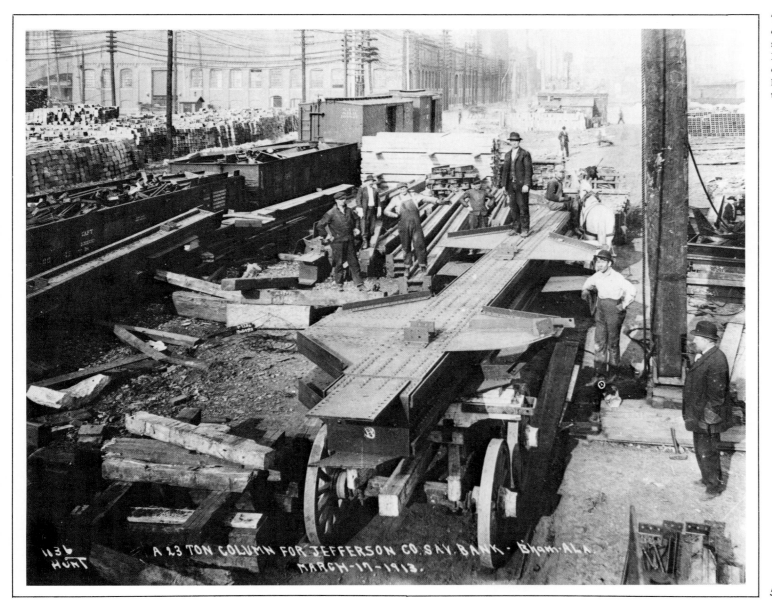

A 23 TON COLUMN FOR JEFFERSON CO. SAV. BANK - B'ham ALA.
MARCH 17 1913.

1136
HUNT

The steel industry partially supplied its own market. The construction of Birmingham and surrounding towns such as Bessemer and Anniston required large quantities of steel. Building a Birmingham bank, 1912. (From the Collections of the Birmingham Public Library)

In addition to mining, the iron and steel industry, and textiles, smaller industries developed throughout the state. In Mobile County investors began a search for oil, hoping to repeat the discoveries of 1901 and 1902 in Texas. They failed. Mobile County, c. 1905. (Wilson Collection, Historic Mobile Preservation Society)

60

This liquid lime sulfur plant was typical of the small industries constructed in the towns of Alabama during the New South era. Thorsby, c. 1895. (Auburn University Archives)

Dependable transportation provided by the state's expanded railways made industrialization possible. By the late 1880s the state's system had been integrated into the national railway network and was carrying Alabama products to regional and national markets. Train on bridge over the Tennessee River near Florence, c. 1890. (Alabama State Department of Archives and History)

While major lines linked the urban regions, smaller lines, sometimes owned by industrial firms, served the specific needs of a number of industries. A logging train crosses the Tallapoosa River at Elmore City, c. 1898. (Alabama State Department of Archives and History)

As the rail system improved, trains replaced river steamers and stagecoaches as the principal passenger carriers. Rail passenger service linked outlying towns to larger cities and cities to one another and to urban areas outside the state. The Louisville and Nashville Railroad Station in Mobile, c. 1905. (Wilson Collection, Historic Mobile Preservation Society)

64

Themselves a major industry, railroads employed thousands of Alabamians such as these firemen in a coal car looking out on the railyards at Tuscaloosa, c. 1895. (Armitstead/Mobile Museum, USA Photo Archives)

Symbol of an era, the locomotive was maintained and repaired by crews in railway shops at locations scattered about the state. The shops of the Louisville and Nashville Railroad in Greenville, c. 1890. (Reynolds Collection, Greenville Public Library)

Large firms, especially in mining, iron and steel, and lumbering, owned and maintained their own locomotives to transport raw materials short distances. Mechanics at the shops of the Creek Mill Company, a Brewton lumber firm, 1904. (McMillan Collection, Brewton)

Black work crews supervised by white foremen built and maintained road beds and track. This crew uses pick and shovel to cut the right of way for the Monte Sano Railway through mountain stone. The railway transported guests the five miles from Huntsville to the mountain resort of Monte Sano. The photograph was taken in the late 1890s. (Auburn University Archives)

BUTTON-HOLE CUT MONTE SANO RAILWAY.

68

Ironically, the railroads made possible the completion of water-transport projects. The crane pictured is lifting stone used in the construction of locks on the Tennessee River at Colbert Shoals near Riverton, 1895. (National Archives)

The construction of canals and locks around the shoals of the Tennessee allowed waterborne traffic to move more freely through the Tennessee Valley and into the Mississippi River system. Federal monies and the work of the U.S. Army Corps of Engineers began a river system that was not completed until the New Deal and the Tennessee Valley Authority. Shown here is lock number six at Muscle Shoals, 1882. (National Archives)

70

Despite navigational difficulties, steamboats plied the Tennessee River throughout the era. *The City of Knoxville* takes on cotton at Decatur sometime in the 1880s. (Alabama State Department of Archives and History)

Although faced with increased competition from railroads during the period, steamboats continued to move goods along the Tombigbee, Black Warrior, and Alabama rivers, all of which fed the port of Mobile. Here the *Sunny South* rides at dockside in Mobile, 1914. (Overbey/Mobile Public Library, USA Photo Archives)

Cotton remained the major cargo and some passengers still traveled by boat between Mobile and such interior river towns as Demopolis and Montgomery. But each year the railroads siphoned off more cargo and passenger trade. The interior of the *Sunny South*, 1914. (Overbey/Mobile Public Library, USA Photo Archives)

In 1915 a series of locks on the Tombig-bee and Black Warrior rivers connected Mobile and Birmingham by water. The lowly barge and tug that transported mineral-region coal and iron products became the workhorses of the waterfront. The river steamer, pictured here at Mobile's cotton docks, c. 1895, gradually faded into oblivion in the years following World War I. (Armitstead/Mobile Museum, USA Photo Archives)

74

Most cargo shipped to foreign ports from Mobile was carried by steamers. The coastal trade, however, saw three- and four-masted sailing vessels remain active throughout the period. This c. 1895 photograph of the Mobile harbor demonstrates the significance of both types of ship to the port. (Armitstead/Mobile Museum, USA Photo Archives)

Whether in town or country the buggy was the favored means of personal transportation. A buggy shop in Huntsville, 1890. (Huntsville Public Library)

Green street   1890   Corner of Green + Lincoln   Clinton

Like the automobiles that followed, the horse and buggy supported a number of related industries, livery, stables, harness shops, blacksmiths, and carriage makers among them. Buggies and harnesses are displayed in Dothan, c. 1890. (G. S. Houston Library, Dothan)

Urban residents rode horse-drawn trolleys during the 1870s and 1880s. In the mineral district surrounding Birmingham, street railways connected several communities. An early trolley system in Oxford, 1885. (Alabama State Department of Archives and History)

Choccolocco St. Oxford Ala. March, 1885.

By the 1890s the electric trolley was replacing the horse-drawn cars and spurring urban and suburban development. These Montgomery cars are parked en masse because company officials refused to obey a city ordinance requiring separate cars for blacks and whites, a proposition they found too expensive. The trolley company compromised on the segregation of individual cars, 1906. (Alabama State Department of Archives and History)

Teams and wagons moved the commodities of urban commerce during most of the era. A majority of the teamsters were black, and some blacks owned trucking firms of considerable size. Mobile teamsters, c. 1900. (Wilson Collection, Historic Mobile Preservation Society)

The coming of the motor truck gradually drove the wagon teamsters out of business. Taken in Mobile about 1910, this photograph depicts that transition. (Mobile Museum Collection)

By the end of the era the automobile had become a prominent factor in urban life. A Mobile dealership, c. 1905. (Wilson Collection, Historic Mobile Preservation Society)

82

Individually owned, practical, and relatively inexpensive, the automobile was quickly integrated into the culture. An orphans' day parade in Mobile, c. 1905. (Wilson Collection, Historic Mobile Preservation Society)

In rural areas poor roads presented a major obstacle to the widespread use of automobiles. This stretch of road between Hurtsboro and Seale in eastern Alabama, 1912, gives a good indication of the condition of most rural roads and shows the typical landscape of the state south of Montgomery. (National Archives)

As autos became more reliable and less expensive they were purchased by rural and small-town residents. The spread of the automobile into the country led to demands for improved roads, a demand quickly endorsed by construction companies, paving contractors, and politicians. This road construction equipment appeared in Huntsville, c. 1915, to promote a "good roads" program. (Alabama State Department of Archives and History)

Industrialization and improved transportation systems resulted in the rapid growth of Alabama's towns and cities. Some, like Anniston and Bessemer, were small industrial towns that owed their existence to mills such as these pictured in the background, Anniston, 1914. Lewis Hine photograph. (Bafford Collection, University of Maryland)

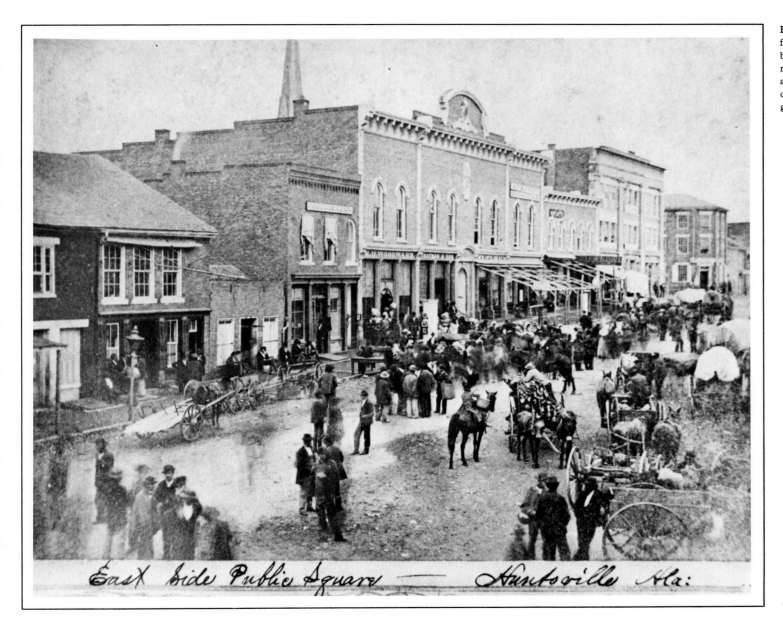

East Side Public Square — Huntsville Ala:

Even the older commercial centers that failed to develop a significant industrial base continued to grow, though at a less rapid pace. Huntsville, shown here as it appeared in 1872, remained a commercial center for the Tennessee Valley region. (Huntsville Public Library)

Other communities developed because of affiliation with state institutions. Auburn, for example, grew from a sleepy agricultural village to a somnolent college town because of the state Agricultural and Mechanical College. This is the center of Auburn, Toomer's corner, 1900. (Auburn University Archives)

The state's three largest urban areas each served different functions. Montgomery served as a commercial center for the surrounding agricultural region, the center of state government, and a river port primarily for the shipment of cotton. Downtown Montgomery, c. 1900. (Alabama State Department of Archives and History)

Mobile, the second largest urban center, remained a commercial community and the state's only gulf port. The city's few industrial firms were small and merchants dominated the economy. Mobile, c. 1910. (Wilson Collection, Historic Mobile Preservation Society)

90

Birmingham was the state's only truly urban industrial center. At the end of the era it was vying with Atlanta and Nashville for prominence among the cities of the New South. The city is pictured here, c. 1915. (Auburn University Archives)

For many Alabamians rapid urbanization created unprecedented opportunities for economic advancement. Projects required to provide water and sewer service, develop adequate transportation systems, and house new commercial and industrial firms employed thousands in the construction industry alone. The men pictured here are construction workers erecting a new post office in Birmingham, 1891. (National Archives)

92

Crews of ditch diggers lay water mains in Mobile under the watchful supervison of their foremen, c. 1900. (Wilson Collection, Historic Mobile Preservation Society)

Workers posed next to a casting, perhaps for a marine steam engine, Mobile, c. 1900. (Overbey/Mobile Public Library, USA Photo Archives)

A result of industrialization, urbanization was also its cause. As they grew, even primarily commercial towns developed factories that produced goods required for expansion and employed a growing industrial work force. Typical of such local industries is the Mobile Veneer Mill pictured here, c. 1900. (Overbey/Mobile Public Library, USA Photo Archives)

Like his Northern counterpart, the Alabama industrial worker found labor in the factory more regulated than that on the farm. A Dothan mechanic with steam engine, c. 1910. (G. S. Houston Library, Dothan)

96

The factory whistle dictated the workday, machines determined the pace of work, and superintendents saw that work was constant. Workers at machines in the Home Industrial Iron Works, Mobile, c. 1900. (Overbey/Mobile Public Library, USA Photo Archives)

Although cotton textile firms were the leading industrial employers of women, women also held a variety of positions in other industries. These women labor in a Mobile print shop, 1906. (Wilson Collection, Historic Mobile Preservation Society)

The use of child labor was also a common phenomenon in many businesses and industries. Children had been viewed as a part of the farm labor force; they continued to be so regarded in the factory and in the city. Lewis Hine photograph of a Mobile newsboy, 1914. (Bafford Collection, University of Maryland)

Although they worked the same long hours, children employed by city commercial or retail firms seldom encountered the regimentation or strenuous physical labor experienced by industrial employees of the same age. A delivery boy for an Opelika store, 1914. Lewis Hine photograph. (Bafford Collection, University of Maryland)

A Montgomery drugstore clerk delivers a soda, 1914. Lewis Hine photograph. (Bafford Collection, University of Maryland)

While every urban community had a transient labor force of those hoping to find regular employment, Mobile had a particularly unstable work force. Sailors from freighters and schooners mingled with crews from riverboats and dockhands along the waterfront. Lumber schooners and their crews, c. 1895. (Armitstead/Mobile Museum, USA Photo Archives)

Sailors on the deck of a freighter, Mobile, c. 1895. (Armitstead/Mobile Museum, USA Photo Archives)

As in other Southern ports, blacks performed the heavy labor of loading and unloading ships. Stevedores at Mobile's banana docks, c. 1895. (Overbey/Mobile Public Library, USA Photo Archives)

In Alabama's two coastal counties many residents made their living from the sea. Fishermen with catch, Mobile, c. 1895. (Armitstead/Mobile Museum, USA Photo Archives)

In every city peddlers hawked a variety of goods, especially foodstuffs. The call of the vegetable man or fish peddler was one of the common sounds of daily urban life. Mobile peddler, c. 1895. (Armitstead/ Mobile Museum, USA Photo Archives)

The growth of cities demanded an expansion of services, which in turn created jobs for a new type of worker, the public servant. Although employed by a private corporation, these Birmingham Traction Company employees provided a quasi-public service, 1896. (From the Collections of the Birmingham Public Library)

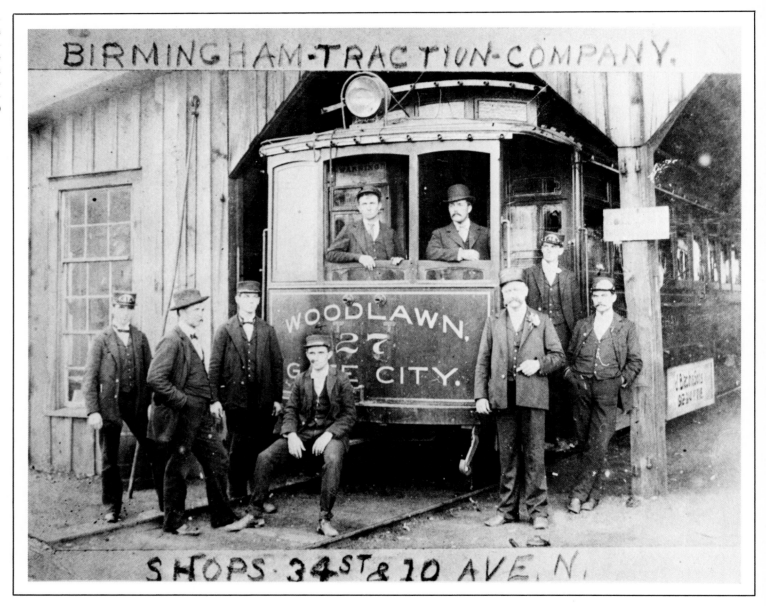

Civil servants had their critics, as demonstrated by this "mounted" policeman, a Mobilian in a Mardi Gras parade costume, c. 1900. Few towns had civil service systems, and as a result the police force was frequently highly political, though professional. (Wilson Collection, Historic Mobile Preservation Society)

Because most homes and businesses were constructed of wood, fires caused frequent and heavy damage, sometimes devastating blocks at a time. To combat such destruction cities and larger towns created professional fire departments, especially in the 1880s. A Huntsville fire company, c. 1895. (Huntsville Public Library)

A fire engine answers an alarm in Dothan, 1908. (G. S. Houston Library, Dothan)

The city offered a variety of services to its residents. These black Mobile barbers and their white customers were photographed in Mobile, c. 1900. Segregation, which was codified in Alabama primarily after 1901, would end this practice. (Wilson Collection, Historic Mobile Preservation Society)

112

Young clerks at a Montgomery drugstore, 1914. Lewis Hine photograph. (Bafford Collection, University of Maryland)

While most of the state's rural residents struggled to earn a livelihood in a depressed agricultural economy, urban merchants expanded their stock to meet the demands of the more affluent city shoppers. These two photographs, both taken in Mobile, c. 1900, reflect the prosperity of the cities. (Overbey/Mobile Public Library, USA Photo Archives)

115

Members of the urban working class had access to more goods and services than were available to the agrarian laborer or tenant. A Mobile grocery, c. 1905. (Wilson Collection, Historic Mobile Preservation Society)

116

The grocery stores pictured on these pages were typical of those in most urban communities. A Dothan firm, c. 1905. (G. S. Houston Library, Dothan)

117

Medical services were readily available to urban residents but the quality of such services was by no means assured. The man pictured here is receiving "electrostatic" treatment, a form of quackery that claimed to cure most of the ills known to man. Mobile, c. 1900. (Wilson Collection, Historic Mobile Preservation Society)

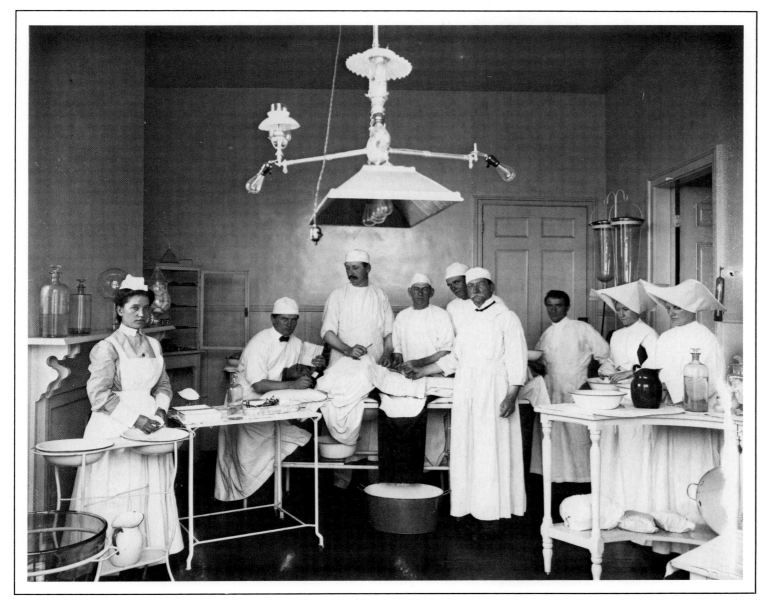

Even the most advanced and respected medical practices were crude. In this portrait of a city hospital operating room, the relatively primitive conditions of early twentieth-century medicine are clear. Mobile, 1904. (Wilson Collection, Historic Mobile Preservation Society)

For the urban resident with some discretionary income, individual or family portraits were available at the photographer's studio. This establishment belonged to W. A. Reed of Mobile, who operated it from the 1870s into the twentieth century. The photograph was probably taken in the late 1880s. (Overbey/Mobile Public Library, USA Photo Archives)

Historians with a camera, commercial photographers in towns all over the state recorded the important personalities and events of their communities. This is a self-portrait of William E. Wilson, a commercial photographer of exceptional ability who set up shop in Mobile in 1895. This remarkable shot reveals Wilson's sense of humor and his awareness of the photograph as a historical document. Surrounded by the tools of his trade, he perches on a barrel of flash powder, which he is about to ignite with his cigar. (Wilson Collection, Historic Mobile Preservation Society)

The Social Setting

Observers of Southern society have often noted the importance of family ties, and Alabamians exhibited a pride in and loyalty to their families. A middle-class urban family, Mobile, c. 1900. (Overbey/Mobile Public Library, USA Photo Archives)

A cotton mill village family from Anniston, 1914. Lewis Hine photograph. (Bafford Collection, University of Maryland)

Families of the rural poor, black or white, faced essentially the same economic realities and in many ways their life-styles were similar. A family from southern Alabama, c. 1905. (Wilson Collection, Historic Mobile Preservation Society)

126

A family from Pike County in southeastern Alabama, c. 1915. (Pike County Collection, USA Photo Archives)

127

As in the rest of the nation, life-styles contrasted sharply in the Alabama of the New South. In urban areas some families lived in lavishly furnished homes, such as the Mobile home pictured here, c. 1885. (Overbey/Mobile Public Library, USA Photo Archives)

The rural poor, especially the tenant, lived in homes constructed of undressed pine boards; some lacked glass windows. This house was photographed in Macon County, c. 1905. (Tuskegee Institute)

The black yeoman farmer lived in a home that differed little from the tenants'. Typical of rural architecture, this home is built in two sections connected by a covered "dog trot." Wilcox County, 1910. (National Archives)

Family recreation often meant outdoor activity, and few activities were as popular as the picnic. This scene captures the essence of the leisure time activities of the upper and middle class. Baldwin County, eastern shore of Mobile Bay, c. 1900. (Wilson Collection, Historic Mobile Preservation Society)

130

Picnickers, probably a church group,
Dothan, c. 1890.
(G. S. Houston Library, Dothan)

Improved rail transportation made resorts more accessible and popular toward the turn of the century. Noccalula Falls, near Gadsden, c. 1890. (Alabama State Department of Archives and History)

In the mountains of north Alabama hotels sprang up to meet the demands of tourists. The Bellevue Hotel, near Gadsden, c. 1890. (Alabama State Department of Archives and History)

Shore resorts were also popular. This group poses on the eastern shore of Mobile Bay, to which large numbers of affluent Mobilians and a few Alabamians from the interior "retired" for much of the summer, c. 1900. (Wilson Collection, Historic Mobile Preservation Society)

Parks provided recreational activities for urban residents, especially the working class. Situated on Mobile Bay and accessible by trolley, Monroe Park offered facilities for swimming, boating, dancing, picnicking, baseball, band concerts, and other events. Photograph c. 1900. (Wilson Collection, Historic Mobile Preservation Society)

135

Birmingham, with its large industrial work force, was the first Alabama city to transport workers to outlying vacation cities. Sponsored by the Salvation Army, this Fresh Air Encampment was held at Pickett's Springs in 1903 for the working women and children of Birmingham. It indicates that Southern Protestant organizations were not entirely oblivious to the concepts of the Social Gospel movement. (Alabama State Department of Archives and History)

136

Excursions by boat were available on the state's interior river systems but were especially popular along the shores of Mobile Bay. Employees of the Southern Gas Company board a bay boat for a company picnic, c. 1915. (Overbey/Mobile Public Library, USA Photo Archives)

Agricultural fairs remained popular events, even in urban areas. Most counties held annual fairs in the fall. The exhibits pictured here were displayed at the state fair held in Birmingham, c. 1915. (Alabama State Department of Archives and History)

138

Sex roles were rigidly stereotyped in the postwar South, more so than in many other parts of the nation. The woman's place was in the home. For many women a visit or club meeting represented the only diversion from housework. Forays into politics would have drawn instant condemnation, for Alabama, like most other Southern states, failed to ratify the women's suffrage amendment to the Constitution. Mobile women, c. 1900. (Overbey/Mobile Public Library, USA Photo Archives)

Children were quickly initiated into their designated social roles. The boy ready for hunting was photographed in Pike County, c. 1915. (Pike County Collection, USA Photo Archives)

140

The photograph of a girl with her dolls and kitten was made in Mobile, c. 1900. (Wilson Collection, Historic Mobile Preservation Society)

For middle-class men, whether in the city or small towns, membership in fraternal and civic organizations was important. Woodmen of the World, Mobile, c. 1905. (Wilson Collection, Historic Mobile Preservation Society)

142

The Red Men ~ circa 1907

Such fraternal groups fostered civic pride, provided social activity, and created an informal setting for business transactions and the exchange of political views. The Red Men of Brewton, 1907. (McMillan Collection, Brewton)

Few events created the excitement that accompanied the arrival of the circus. An exotic transient, the circus stirred the imagination of Alabamians in cities and small villages alike. The Queen City Circus in Marion, 1872, whose side show sign "OUR MOTTO—MORALITY" captured the Victorian attitudes of the era. (Brantley Collection, Samford)

144

Balloon ascensions were frequent attractions at fairs and other special events. A balloonist at an Opelika street fair, c. 1890. (Auburn University Archives)

Tinkers and inventors were abundant in a society fascinated by the machine, and Southerners were as fascinated as residents in the rest of the nation. This flying machine was constructed by John Fowler of Mobile soon after the Wright brothers made their first flight. Photo c. 1905. (Wilson Collection, Historic Mobile Preservation Society)

146

The appearance of an airplane before World War I was an event sure to attract a crowd. This "pusher" plane with its curious admirers was photographed in Georgiana in 1912. (McMillan Collection, Brewton)

While airplanes captured the imagination of the adventurous, the horse and buggy furnished transportation for most Alabamians throughout the era. Ownership of a fine horse and buggy indicated some wealth and social standing. Mobile, c. 1900. (Wilson Collection, Historic Mobile Preservation Society)

For the rural poor, transportation meant a ride on a mule, the animal they were most likely to own. Pike County, c. 1915. (Pike County Collection, USA Photo Archives)

By the end of the era the automobile was beginning to replace the horse and buggy, even in rural areas. These men exhibit an obvious pride in the automobile they surround. Pike County, c. 1915. (Pike County Collection, USA Photo Archives)

Although it became the best known of the urban festivals of the period, Mardi Gras was not a part of Mobile's antebellum heritage. Begun in 1868 it soon dominated the port city's social life. Birmingham unsuccessfully attempted to establish a Mardi Gras carnival in the 1890s. Both carnivals represented efforts of a defeated people to celebrate what they saw as a glorious past. This court and these floats appeared in a Mobile Mardi Gras early in this century. Above: (Overbey/Mobile Public Library, USA Photo Archives)

152

(Wilson Collection, Historic Mobile Preservation Society)

Militia units staged another popular form of celebrating the past. They represented their communities in state, regional, and national drill competitions and mock battles that kept alive the spirit of the "Lost Cause." Mobile's Lomax Rifles, 1904. (Wilson Collection, Historic Mobile Preservation Society)

Often open by invitation only and named for former Confederate companies, the militia units were among Alabama's most influential social organizations. Two members of the Montgomery Greys, c. 1885. (Alabama State Department of Archives and History)

The Civil War overcame but did not erase the loyalty of Alabamians to the nation. While most postwar Alabamians glorified the Lost Cause, they also celebrated their national heritage. These Ensley children are pictured en route to a Fourth of July picnic, c. 1905. (Alabama State Department of Archives and History)

Crowds celebrate the centennial of the founding of St. Stephens, the first American town in Alabama. Established by settlers in southwest Alabama, the town had ceased to exist by the time of the centennial. Site of St. Stephens, 1899. (Alabama State Department of Archives and History)

Postwar presidential visits encouraged Southerners to hope for acceptance as Americans by the rest of the nation and were interpreted as signs that the wounds of war had healed. Theodore Roosevelt's visit to Tuskegee in 1905, pictured here, also underscored the importance of Booker T. Washington in Republican politics. (Tuskegee Institute)

As the first Southerner elected president since Zachary Taylor, Woodrow Wilson received a tumultuous welcome in Alabama and throughout the South. To many he symbolized the true end of Reconstruction and the return of Southern Democrats to national prominence. Here Wilson enters Mobile, 1913. (Mobile Museum Collection)

159

On the antebellum plantation Christmas had been a two-week vacation between the harvest and the preparation for spring planting, in addition to being the most important religious holiday. As urban communities developed in the South, Christmas remained a family holiday and retained most of its antebellum traditions. This is a Mobile family on Christmas day, c. 1900. (Wilson Collection, Historic Mobile Preservation Society)

A Christmas party for Mobile's orphans sponsored by the Salvation Army, c. 1910. (Overbey/Mobile Public Library, USA Photo Archives)

161

Team sports became popular during the era, especially in urban centers, but were almost exclusively for boys. The Ensley High School basketball team, 1910. (Alabama State Department of Archives and History)

162

Bloomers allowed girls to participate in sports in an era when modesty was more important than athletic performance. The girls' basketball team of Baker's Academy, a private Mobile school, c. 1900. (Overbey/Mobile Public Library, USA Photo Archives)

The long Alabama summers enhanced the appeal of baseball and most communities had organized teams. In rural areas men and boys gathered on weekends for impromptu contests staged in open fields. Here is the team of Wright's Academy, Mobile, c. 1900. (Overbey/Mobile Public Library, USA Photo Archives)

Football became a fixture of collegiate life during the 1890s but was not a popular playground "pick up" sport. The college teams, however, received the same adulation as teams all across the country. The Agricultural and Mechanical College, Auburn, team of 1893. (Auburn University Archives)

Whether engaged in the traditional fox hunt or the rowdy night hunts for 'coon or 'possum, Alabama males reveled in the excitement of the chase. The poorest tenant enjoyed stalking small game, although he often did so to put meat on the family table. Alabama bear hunters and their prize, 1914. (Overbey/Mobile Public Library, USA Photo Archives)

166

Fishing possessed the same universal appeal and some fishermen went to great lengths to record their catch. These anglers carried their fish to the studio to be photographed. Mobile, c. 1900. (Wilson Collection, Historic Mobile Preservation Society)

167

A leisurely outing to a nearby creek was an acceptable recreational activity for women, including those of the upper class in south Alabama, c. 1900. (Wilson Collection, Historic Mobile Preservation Society)

Inexpensive, cooling, and fun, swimming was the ideal summer sport. In rural areas such as this south Alabama location, the sport was practiced with few formalities, c. 1900. (Wilson Collection, Historic Mobile Preservation Society)

While classical music was performed infrequently even in the larger cities, the influence of folk music was pervasive. In this photograph loggers at Yellow Pine in southwestern Alabama relax after a day's labor, c. 1895. (Armitstead/Mobile Museum, USA Photo Archives)

170

Many communities supported bands that reflected intense community pride and the desire for "progress." Babbitry and boosterism were as common in Alabama as in Ohio, in towns small and large, as the banner of the Bay Minette band indicates. Photograph by Ort Ertzinger, c. 1917. (Lindsey Collection, Bay Minette)

Poverty and low educational levels combined to deny the pleasures of the performing arts to all but a few of the state's urban residents. Amateur players in *As You Like It*, Anniston, 1904. (Alabama State Department of Archives and History)

Except for vaudeville shows, professional players were seen infrequently. Pickert's Opera Company in Mobile, c. 1900. (Wilson Collection, Historic Mobile Preservation Society)

For many Alabamians a trip to the city was a once-a-year event and one of the highlights of their social activity. One of the state's early department stores, Gayfer's of Mobile, c. 1910. (Overbey/Mobile Public Library, USA Photo Archives)

174

Downtown retail centers served both urban residents and shoppers from outlying rural communities. A Dothan hardware store, c. 1908. (G. S. Houston Library, Dothan)

Motion pictures provided urban residents with more than entertainment. Filmed at central locations and distributed nationally, they made Alabamians aware of national events and cultural trends. Mobile, c. 1905. (Wilson Collection, Historic Mobile Preservation Society)

176

Restaurants and delicatessens added a bit of elegance to urban life, but most were beyond the economic means of all but a few. Planters' Cafe, Mobile, c. 1900. (Overbey/Mobile Public Library, USA Photo Archives)

The saloon was a fixture of urban life until temperance forces obtained the passage of prohibition legislation in 1907 and again in 1914. A Birmingham saloon, 1891. (From the Collections of the Birmingham Public Library)

178

Three men hoist their mugs outside the Happy Holler Saloon, Coden, c. 1905. This scene would soon change. For years after prohibition, Alabamians would vote dry while manufacturing large quantities of corn whiskey. (Wilson Collection, Historic Mobile Preservation Society)

Along the gulf, hurricanes struck with devastating force and between 1890 and 1920 with some regularity. Damage at the wharf, 1916. (Overbey/Mobile Public Library, USA Photo Archives)

Hurricane damage in downtown Mobile, 1916. (Mobile Museum Collection)

No institution played a larger role in Southern life than did the church, and for most Alabamians the church was Protestant. St. Luke's Episcopal Church, Jacksonville, 1871. (Brantley Collection, Samford)

182

With its blend of militant evangelical Protestantism and social consciousness, the Salvation Army captured the essence of the Christian theology of most Alabamians. Here the Salvation Army sponsors a born-again Christmas party in Mobile, c. 1900. (Wilson Collection, Historic Mobile Preservation Society)

Like the white population, most blacks were either Baptist or Methodist. Their religious practices, though sometimes perhaps more exuberant, differed little from those of white churches. For members of both races, for example, baptism was a social and religious event. A baptism in a south Alabama stream, c. 1900. (Wilson Collection, Historic Mobile Preservation Society)

NEGRO BAPTIZING   MOBILE ALA.

184

The Sunday morning church service was the high point of the week for many Alabamians. The church pictured here stood in Macon County, c. 1910. (Tuskegee Institute)

Though small, Alabama's Catholic community was larger than that of most Southern states. Confined largely to the Gulf Coast and the Birmingham area, it encountered increased hostility in north Alabama with the revival of the state Ku Klux Klan in 1916, especially in Birmingham. In south Alabama where the church was a part of the colonial heritage, it continued unmolested. Laying the cornerstone of St. Margaret's Church, Bayou la Batre, 1908. (Mobile Museum Collection)

The society's preoccupation with the racial issue spared the state's small Jewish population from overt anti-Semitism. Largely urban, the Jewish community was influential in most areas of city life, including politics. A confirmation class with rabbi, Mobile, 1908. (Overbey/Mobile Public Library, USA Photo Archives)

Though religion eased the sorrow, Alabamians saw death strike down the young all too frequently. At death, the body was "laid out" in the home and relatives and friends gathered for the "setting up." There family ties and a shared religious faith made possible the acceptance of life's brevity. Young woman "laid out" in Mobile, c. 1906. (Wilson Collection, Historic Mobile Preservation Society)

Childbirth, childhood diseases, and a lack of medical facilities brought an early death to many young women and children. Families were fortunate to escape the death of a child. Mobile, c. 1905. (Wilson Collection, Historic Mobile Preservation Society)

For the majority of the state's rural population, educational opportunities were minimal. Prior to the Progressive movement, one-room schools staffed by poorly trained and underpaid teachers were open less than four months a year. High rates of illiteracy were the predictable results. An old school in Lexington in north Alabama, 1911. (Alabama State Department of Archives and History)

190

The Progressive era saw major educational reforms, including longer terms, revised curricula, and improved facilities. A new school in Cleburne County in northeast Alabama, 1911. (Alabama State Department of Archives and History)

A holdover from the antebellum era, the private academy provided the children of the more affluent an adequate, and sometimes excellent, secondary education while steeping them in the "Southern tradition." Cadets of the Mobile Military Institute, c. 1900. (Wilson Collection, Historic Mobile Preservation Society)

192

Although some mill villages established schools earlier, most did so only after progressive legislation required that instruction be made available to all child laborers. The law required an eight-week school term. Huntsville textile mill village school, 1913. Lewis Hine photograph. (Bafford Collection, University of Maryland)

193

Capstone of the state's higher educational system, the University of Alabama responded to public pressures and developed educational programs as well as the traditional liberal arts curriculum. Teaching teachers in a summer school reading program at the University, 1916. (University of Alabama)

194

At Auburn, the state Agricultural and Mechanical College trained young men for careers in the growing industrial economy and taught the virtues of scientific agriculture. Its rapid development was perhaps the major achievement of the agrarian reformers of the 1890s. An Auburn chemistry class, 1893. (Auburn University Archives)

Opened in 1896, the Alabama Girls' Industrial School at Montevallo was to instruct white girls in industrial and scientific subjects. Such instruction was alien to the Southern view of the role of women and the school became primarily a teachers' college. Photo c. 1900. (Alabama State Department of Archives and History)

Although the University of Alabama began to admit a few coeds in 1893, before the Girls' Industrial School opened only normal schools offered a real opportunity for higher education to women. By 1900 the state operated seven normal schools, five for whites and two for blacks. The faculty of the normal school at Troy, 1900. Note the averted gaze of all the female faculty. (Alabama State Department of Archives and History)

197

Professional education was reserved for whites. These young men made up the 1905 class of the Medical School of Alabama, which was in Mobile. (Overbey/Mobile Public Library, USA Photo Archives)

198

The most famous of Alabama's private institutions, Booker T. Washington's Tuskegee Institute taught blacks "practical" skills. Often criticized for emphasizing craft training, Washington nevertheless attempted to provide Southern blacks with the economic foundations Reconstruction had failed to develop. Young men in Tuskegee's harness shop, c. 1905. (Tuskegee Institute)

199

For most of the New South era, a coalition of Bourbon Democrats dedicated to industrial progress and the interests of the planter class controlled the political fortunes of the state. The Alabama House of Representatives, 1892. (Alabama State Department of Archives and History)

Firmly in command of the election process, the Bourbons beat back the challenge mounted by agrarian reformers in the early 1890s through the use of fraud, racial fears, and a captive black vote. The Alabama Senate, 1892. (Alabama State Department of Archives and History)

The racial issue permeated every aspect of life in Alabama and the South. Organizations such as the United Daughters of the Confederacy, pictured here celebrating the return of a captured Confederate battle flag, continued to defend the plantation life. Selma, 1897. (Alabama State Department of Archives and History)

Though free, blacks remained at the bottom of the society's economic and social order. Some were employed in the trades, but most worked as common laborers, domestics, or tenant farmers. A lady of the house with domestic servants, Mobile, c. 1900. (Wilson Collection, Historic Mobile Preservation Society)

203

Imposed by custom in many areas of life soon after the Civil War, segregation was rigidly codified in the late nineteenth and early twentieth centuries. A segregated clinic of the Tennessee Coal and Iron Company, a holding of United States Steel, Docena, 1917. (From the Collections of the Birmingham Public Library)

204

The absurdities of segregation are proclaimed by the slogan of the Imperial Laundry, Birmingham, 1908. (From the Collections of the Birmingham Public Library)

Booker T. Washington's policies of social segregation and reliance upon the "best whites" to encourage economic and educational opportunities for blacks are illustrated by these photographs, both taken by Frances B. Johnston at the celebration of Tuskegee's twenty-fifth anniversary in 1906. White philanthropists watch the Tuskegee faculty pass in review. (Tuskegee Institute)

Tuskegee thrived on donations from Northern capitalists, who saw industrial education both as an answer to the race question and as the appropriate form of education for the working class, regardless of race. Tuskegee students serve visiting dignitaries. (Tuskegee Institute)

Well before the advent of legal segregation, Alabama's criminal code fell more heavily upon blacks. Black felons were leased by the state to railroads, mines, and other firms in need of unskilled labor. Although white convicts were also leased, blacks invariably made up a large majority of the convict labor force. Prison warden and dogs, Sprague Junction, south of Montgomery, c. 1900. (Alabama State Department of Archives and History)

Warden Jackson & His man-hunters Ready For the Chase.
Sprague Junction, Ala—

Jail ~ Ardilla Ala

During this era antiblack sentiments reached their height. Lynchings were not uncommon and blacks lived in fear of violence for themselves and their families. Prisoners held at gunpoint in a rural jail near Ardilla, 1912. (G. S. Houston Library, Dothan)

Northern whites often shared Southern racial attitudes. "Uncle Matt," pictured here in 1898 at his Huntsville home, was adopted as a mascot by a company of New York troops stationed in the city during the Spanish-American War. The photograph was taken to sell to tourists as an example of the "quaintness" of Southern blacks. (Huntsville Public Library)

The fact that black troops were stationed in Huntsville and other Southern towns during the Spanish-American War revived memories of Reconstruction and stirred the flames of racial hatred. Two members of the Tenth Cavalry, a unit that had performed with valor in Cuba, were killed while stationed in Huntsville. Photo taken in Huntsville, 1898. (Huntsville Public Library)

Although the Spanish-American War aroused racial feelings, it was popular with Alabamians who saw it as an opportunity to prove their loyalty to the nation. President McKinley shrewdly recognized Southern patriotism by appointing former Confederate General and long-term Alabama Congressman Joseph Wheeler a major general in the American army. Wheeler, mounted on a horse in the foreground, reviews troops in Huntsville, 1898. (Huntsville Public Library)

The original New South era ended with Alabamians still seeking national acceptance and hoping to find it in the surge of patriotism that accompanies war. The coming of World War I again allowed them to demonstrate their allegiance to the Union while retaining their loyalty to the military tradition of the Lost Cause. A Liberty Bond parade in Mobile during World War I. (Overbey/Mobile Public Library, USA Photo Archives)

213

Bibliographic Essay

Most of the books and articles listed in this bibliographic essay can be found in the collections of larger public libraries. A few must be obtained from the more specialized collections of major research libraries, such as those at The University of Alabama or Auburn University. This essay is not intended to be exhaustive and contains only published works. It is designed to suggest to the general reader additional material about each of the many subjects covered by the photographs contained in this volume.

Two general works essential for further study of Alabama in the New South era are C. Vann Woodward, *Origins of the New South, 1877–1913* (Baton Rouge, 1971), and George B. Tindall, *The Emergence of the New South, 1913–1945* (Baton Rouge, 1967). The most recent general history of Alabama is Daniel S. Gray and J. Barton Starr, *Alabama: A Place, A People, A Point of View* (Dubuque, Iowa, 1977). Albert B. Moore's *History of Alabama* (University, Alabama, 1934) is still useful. Lucille B. Griffith's edited work, *Alabama: A Documentary History to 1900* (University, Alabama, 1972), is indispensable for the beginning student of the state's history, as is Virginia V. Hamilton's highly readable account, *Alabama, A Bicentennial History* (New York, 1977).

Among the many works that examine Alabama's postwar agricultural economy, Jonathan M. Wiener, *Social Origins of the New South, Alabama, 1860–1885* (Baton Rouge, 1978), is required reading, although very controversial. Pete Daniels, *The Shadow of Slavery: Peonage in the South, 1901–1969* (Urbana, Illinois, 1972), and Daniel A. Novak, *The Wheel of Servitude, Black Forced Labor After Slavery* (Lexington, Kentucky, 1978), portray the agrarian labor system. A more positive interpretation of the role of the freedmen in the agricultural work force is found in Roger Ransom and Richard Sutch, *One Kind of Freedom: The Economic Consequences of Emancipation* (New York, 1977). Two articles by Glenn N. Sisk, "Rural Merchandizing in the Alabama Black Belt, 1875–1917," *Journal of Farm Economics* 37 (1955):705–15, and "The Wholesale Commission Business in the Alabama Black Belt, 1875–1917," ibid. 38 (1956):799–802, detail the operation of the agricultural credit system, as does Margaret P. Farmer, "Furnishing Merchants and Sharecroppers in Pike County, Alabama," *Alabama Review* 23 (1970):143–51. Grady McWhiney, "The Revolution in Nineteenth-Century Alabama Agricul-

ture," *Alabama Review* 31 (1978): 3–32, presents a brief summary of agricultural developments within the state.

Except for Richard W. Massey, Jr., "Logging Railroads in Alabama, 1880–1914," *Alabama Review* 14 (1961):41–50, little has been written about the state's lumber industry. The textile industry, however, has received more attention. Among the many articles on that subject are Frank C. Bennett, "The Old Mill: The Anniston Manufacturing Company, 1880–1959," *Cotton History Review* 1 (1960):13–18; Will Mickle, "Huntsville, Alabama: Cotton Textile Center of the New South," ibid.:92–102; Peter A. Brannon, "Donald Comer, Dean of the Alabama Textile Industry," ibid.:119–21; and William G. Irby, "The Avondale Mills of Alabama and Georgia," *Textile History Review* 3 (1962):197–204.

Ethel M. Armes, *The Story of Coal and Iron in Alabama* (Birmingham, 1910), is still the best published study of these related industries. Her work is supplemented by several articles by Justin Fuller, including "Notes and Documents: Alabama Business Leaders, 1865–1900," *Alabama Review* 16 and 17 (1963 and 1964):279–86 and 63–75; "From Iron to Steel: Alabama's Industrial Evolution," ibid. 17 (1964):137–48; and "Boom Towns and Blast Furnaces: Town Promotion in Alabama, 1885–1893," ibid. 29 (1976):37–48. Robert H. McKenzie has two articles on the early iron industry, "Reconstruction of the Alabama Iron Industry," *Alabama Review* 25 (1972):178–91, and "Horace Ware: Alabama Iron Pioneer," ibid. 26 (1973):157–72. Grace Hooten Gates, "Anniston: Model City and Rival City," *Alabama Review* 31 (1978):33–47; Marlene H. Rikard, "George Gordon Crawford: Man of the New South," ibid. 31 (1978):163–81; and John B. Ryan, Jr., "Willard Warner, and the Rise and Fall of the Iron Industry, in Tecumseh, Alabama," ibid. 24 (1971):261-79, are also helpful.

Alabama's railway systems are treated in a number of studies. Maury Klein, *History of the Louisville and Nashville Railroad* (New York, 1972), provides an excellent study of Alabama's most important rail line. Articles on Alabama's railroads are plentiful. Two articles by James Doster, "Trade Centers and Railroad Rates in Alabama, 1873–1885; The Case of Greenville, Montgomery and Opelika," *Journal of Southern History* 18 (1952): 169–92, and "Wetumpka's Railroad: Its Construction and Early Traffic," *Alabama Review* 3 (1950):174–82, combine with Glenn N. Sisk, "Railroad Development in Alabama: The Black Belt, 1875–1917," National Railway Historical Society *Bulletin* 20 (1955):8–12; Michael J. Dunn III, "The Birmingham and Southeastern Railroad," *Alabama Historical Quarterly* 27 (1965):59–79; Dudley S. Johnson, "Early History of the Alabama Midland Railroad Company," *Alabama Review* 21 (1968):276–87; and Jean E. Keith, "Sand Mountains and Sawgrass Marshes," ibid. 7

(1954):99–112, to give an excellent picture of the state's railway systems. James Doster's *Railroads in Alabama Politics, 1875–1914* (University, Alabama, 1957), is the definitive study of that subject.

The literature on other transportation systems is, for the most part, yet to be written. Three articles by Glenn N. Sisk, "Steamboat Days in the Alabama Black Belt, 1875–1917," *Steamboat Bill of Facts* 13 (1956):1–4; " 'Good Roads' and Bad in the Alabama Black Belt—1875–1915," *Antique Automobile* 20 (1956):25–26; and "Automobiles and Road Building in the Alabama Black Belt After 1900," ibid. 21 (1957):22–23, constitute an important body of work on the subject. Complementing Sisk's articles are a work by John Goodrum and others, *Rivers of Alabama* (Huntsville, 1968), and an early but still useful work, William E. Martin, *Internal Improvements in Alabama* (Baltimore, 1902).

Historians have only begun to record the story of Alabama's non-agrarian work force. Melton A. McLaurin, *The Knights of Labor in the South* (Westport, Connecticut, 1978); Robert D. Ward and William W. Rogers, *Labor Revolt in Alabama; The Great Strike of 1894* (University, Alabama, 1965); and Elizabeth H. Davidson, *Child Labor Legislation in the Southern Textile States* (Chapel Hill, 1931), are among the few books on the subject. Blacks in the labor force are the subject of Herbert G. Gutman, "Black Coal Miners and the Greenback-Labor Party in Redeemer Alabama, 1878–1879," *Labor History* 10 (1969):506–35, and Paul B. Worthman, "Black Workers and Labor Unions in Birmingham, Alabama, 1897–1904," ibid.:375–407. Wayne Flynt, "Alabama White Protestantism and Labor, 1900–1914," *Alabama Review* 25 (1972):192–217, examines the relationship between progressivism and labor reform, as does Hugh C. Bailey, *Edgar Gardner Murphy: Gentle Progressive* (Coral Gables, Florida, 1968).

There is no work on the urbanization of Alabama, and few good histories of its major cities. Birmingham has a number of histories. George M. Cruikshank, *A History of Birmingham and its Environs* (Chicago, 1920), 2 vols., and John R. Harnady, *The Book of Birmingham* (New York, 1921), contain useful material, but Carl Harris, *Political Power in Birmingham, 1871–1921* (Knoxville, Tennessee, 1977), is the best work available. The best work on Mobile is Charles G. Summersell, *Mobile: History of a Seaport Town* (University, Alabama, 1949), although Caldwell Delaney, ed., *Craighead's Mobile: Being the Fugitive Writings of Erwin S. Craighead and Frank Craighead* (Mobile, 1968); Erwin Craighead, *From Mobile's Past* (Mobile, 1925); and, by the same author, *Mobile, Fact and Tradition* (Mobile, 1930), should be consulted. Except for Mary Ann Neeley, "Montgomery, 1885–1887: The Years of Jubilee," *Alabama Review* 32 (1979):108–18, there is little to be found on that city. Claude C.

Grayson, *Yesterday and Today, Memories of Selma and its People* (New York, 1948), and John Knox and William H. Jenkins, *The Story of Decatur, Alabama* (Decatur, 1970), provide material on important Alabama regional urban centers. Visual histories exist for the state's two largest cities: Malcolm C. McMillan, *Yesterday's Birmingham* (Miami, Florida, 1975), and Michael Thomason and Melton A. McLaurin, *Mobile: American River City* (Mobile, 1975).

The state's social history has been seriously neglected and offers a fertile field of investigation for a new generation of historians. Almost nothing has been done on the life of the average citizen. Paul Worthman, "Working Class Mobility in Birmingham, Alabama, 1880–1914," in *Anonymous Americans*, ed. Tamara K. Harever (Englewood Cliffs, New Jersey, 1971), provides an example of the kinds of studies that should be made. Other important articles are Martha M. Bigelow, "Birmingham's Carnival of Crime, 1871–1910," *Alabama Review* 3 (1950):123–33, and Glenn N. Sisk, "Crime and Justice in the Alabama Black Belt, 1875–1917," *Mid-America* 40 (1958):106–13. Sisk has two other important articles, "Social Life in the Alabama Black Belt, 1875–1917," *Alabama Review* 8 (1955):83–103, and "Social Classes in the Alabama Black Belt, 1870–1910," *Alabama Historical Quarterly* 20 (1958):653–55. William W. Rogers, "The Alabama State Fair, 1865–1900," *Alabama Review* 11 (1958):100–116, chronicles the development of a significant educational and social institution.

A number of works explore the multifaceted and vigorous religious life of postwar Alabama. Protestant denominations are represented by Wayne Flynt, "Religion in the Urban South: The Divided Religious Mind of Birmingham, 1900–1930," *Alabama Review* 30 (1977):108–34; Daniel L. Cloyd, "Prelude to Reform: Political, Economic, and Social Thought of Alabama Baptists, 1877–1890," ibid. 31 (1978):48–64; and Glenn N. Sisk, "Churches in the Alabama Black Belt, 1875–1917," *Church History* 23 (1954):153–74. The black church is examined in Stevenson N. Ried, *History of Colored Baptists in Alabama* (Gadsden, Alabama, 1949), and Glenn N. Sisk, "Negro Churches in the Alabama Black Belt, 1875–1917," *Journal of the Presbyterian Historical Society* 33 (1955):87–92. Alabama's Catholic heritage is explored in Oscar H. Lipscomb, *The Administration of John Quinlan, Second Bishop of Mobile, 1859–1883* (Philadelphia, 1968), and Aloysius Plaisance, "Benedictine Monks in Alabama, 1876–1956," *Alabama Review* 11 (1958):56–63. Mark H. Elovitz, *A Century of Jewish Life in Dixie: The Birmingham Experience* (University, Alabama, 1974), is the best work on the state's small Jewish community.

Among several works on education, two are essential reading: Oscar W. Hyatt, *The Development of Secondary Education in Alabama Prior to*

1920 (Nashville, 1933), and Horace M. Bond, *Negro Education in Alabama, A Study in Cotton and Steel* (Washington, 1939). Supplementing these studies are Robert G. Sherer, *Subordination or Liberation? The Development of Conflicting Theories of Black Education in Nineteenth Century Alabama* (University, Alabama, 1977); Kenneth Johnson, "The Peabody Fund: Its Role and Influence in Alabama," *Alabama Review* 27 (1974):101–26; Glenn N. Sisk, "The Educational Awakening in Alabama and Its Effect Upon the Black Belt, 1900–1917," *Journal of Negro Education* 25 (1956):191–96, and "White Private Schools in Alabama, 1875–1900," *Peabody Education Journal* 32 (1955):295–99; and Irving Gershenberg, "The Negro and the Development of White Public Education in the South; Alabama, 1880–1930," *Journal of Negro Education* 39 (1970):50–59.

The development of higher education is recorded in a number of institutional histories. James B. Sellers, *History of the University of Alabama* (University, 1953), and Ralph B. Draughon, *Alabama Polytechnic Institute* (New York, 1954), chronicle the rise of the state's two major institutions. Other works include E. M. Schackelford, *The First Fifty Years of the State Teachers College at Troy, Alabama* (Montgomery, 1937); Rhoda C. Ellison, *History of Huntingdon College, 1854–1954* (University, Alabama, 1954); Richard W. Griffin, "Athens College: The Middle Years, 1873–1914," *Methodist History* 4 (1965):46–58; and Howard L. Holley, "Medical Education in Alabama," *Alabama Review* 7 (1954):245–64.

The literature on race relations is voluminous; that on Booker T. Washington alone would make up a lengthy bibliography. The best comprehensive biography of Washington is Samuel R. Spencer, Jr., *Booker T. Washington and the Negro's Place in American Life* (Boston, 1955). Louis R. Harlan, *Booker T. Washington—the Making of a Black Leader, 1856–1901* (New York, 1972), is the first volume of a projected multivolume biography that will undoubtedly become the standard work when completed. Booker T. Washington's autobiography, *Up From Slavery* (New York, 1901), remains essential, and exciting, reading.

Although Washington dominates the literature on race relations in the postwar era, a number of articles explore other topics. Disenfranchisement is considered in Joseph H. Taylor, "Populism and Disenfranchisement in Alabama," *Journal of Negro History* 34 (1949):410–27, and David A. Bagwell, "The 'Magical Process': The Sayre Election Law of 1893," *Alabama Review* 25 (1972):83–104. Other significant articles include Glenn N. Sisk, "Negro Migration in the Alabama Black Belt, 1875–1917," *Negro History Bulletin* 17 (November 1953):32–34, and Alfred W. Reyn-

olds, "The Alabama Negro Colony in Mexico, 1894–1896," *Alabama Review* 5 and 6 (1952 and 1953):243–68 and 31–58.

The attitudes of Alabamians of the New South toward war can be gained from two works: Sergeant M. Koeningsberg, *Southern Martyrs: A History of Alabama's White Regiments During the Spanish-American War* (Montgomery, 1898), and Richard G. Eaves, "Pro-Allied Sentiment in Alabama, 1914–1917," *Alabama Review* 25 (1972):30–55.

Although this study avoids politics, the subject cannot be entirely ignored. Literature on the subject is not lacking, but three works cover the era nicely. The three are Allen J. Going, *Bourbon Democracy in Alabama, 1874–1890* (University, Alabama, 1957); William W. Rogers, *The One Gallused Rebellion: Agrarianism in Alabama, 1865–1896* (Baton Rouge, 1970); and Sheldon Hackney, *Populism to Progressivism in Alabama* (Princeton, 1969).

Index

of Photographic Collections

Alabama State Department of Archives and History, Montgomery, Alabama, xiv, xix, 18, 19, 26, 31, 32, 50, 51, 62, 63, 71, 78, 79, 85, 89, 132, 133, 136, 138, 155, 156, 157, 162, 172, 190, 191, 196, 197, 200, 201, 202, 208

T. E. Armitstead/Museum of the City of Mobile Collection, University of South Alabama (USA) Photographic Archives, Mobile, Alabama, xx, 24, 25, 30, 41, 43, 44, 47, 65, 74, 75, 102, 103, 104, 105, 106, 107, 170

Auburn University Archives, Auburn, Alabama, 21, 27, 38, 39, 61, 68, 88, 91, 145, 165, 195

Bafford Photography Collection, University of Maryland Baltimore County Library, Baltimore, Maryland, 46, 48, 49, 52, 86, 99, 100, 101, 113, 125, 193

Birmingham Public Library, Department of Archives and Manuscripts, Birmingham, Alabama, 54, 55, 58, 59, 108, 178, 204, 205

William H. Brantley, Jr., Collection, Special Collections Division, Samford University Library, Birmingham, Alabama, 34, 35, 144, 182

Harper Collection, Samford University Library, Birmingham, Alabama, 57

George S. Houston Memorial Library, Dothan, Alabama, 36, 37, 77, 96, 111, 117, 131, 175, 209

Huntsville-Madison County Public Library, Huntsville, Alabama, 76, 87, 110, 149, 210, 211, 212

Walter M. Lindsey Collection, Bay Minette, Alabama, 171

Ed Leigh McMillan Collection, Brewton, Alabama, 67, 143, 147

Eunivay B. Mills Collection, Brewton, Alabama, 42

Museum of the City of Mobile, Mobile, Alabama, 81, 159, 181, 186

National Archives, Washington, D.C., 69, 70, 84, 92, 129

Erik Overbey Collection donated by the Mobile Public Library, University of South Alabama (USA) Photographic Archives, Mobile, Alabama, x, xiii, xvi, 72, 73, 94, 95, 97, 104, 114, 115, 120, 124, 128, 137, 139, 152, 161, 163, 164, 166, 174, 177, 180, 187, 198, 213

Thomas Duke Parke Papers, Department of Archives and Manuscripts, Birmingham Public Library, Birmingham, Alabama, 55

Pike County Museum Association Collection, University of South Alabama (USA) Photographic Archives, Mobile, Alabama, xi, xii, xviii, 127, 140, 150, 151

Erskine Ramsey Papers, Department of Archives and Manuscripts, Birmingham Public Library, Birmingham, Alabama, 54

William Peyton Reynolds Collection, Greenville Public Library, Greenville, Alabama, 66

Tuskegee Institute Archives, Tuskegee, Alabama, xv, xvii, 20, 22, 23, 29, 129, 158, 185, 199, 206, 207

University of Alabama Library, Photographic Collection, W. S. Hoole Special Collections Library, University, Alabama, 53, 194

University of Alabama in Birmingham, Center for Urban Affairs, Birmingham, Alabama, 56

William E. Wilson Collection, Historic Mobile Preservation Society, Mobile, Alabama, 28, 33, 40, 45, 60, 64, 80, 82, 83, 90, 93, 98, 109, 112, 116, 118, 119, 121, 126, 130, 134, 135, 141, 142, 146, 148, 153, 154, 160, 167, 168, 169, 173, 176, 179, 183, 184, 188, 189, 192, 203, 220